Klasse 5

**Laurence Harger
Terry Moston
Malcolm Sexton**

Langenscheidt-Longman
ENGLISH LANGUAGE TEACHING

westermann

English live
für das 5. Schuljahr

Autoren:
Laurence Harger
Terry Moston
Malcolm Sexton

Mitarbeiter:
Waldemar Bindseil, Soltau
Prof. Dr. Wolf-Dietrich Bald, Universität Köln
Dr. Werner Kieweg, Universität München
Adolf Schwarz, Eichenau
Anne Wichmann-Jones, Lancaster University
Celine Sawicki, Münster

Beratende Mitwirkung:
Maria Kieweg, Schwabmünchen
Ursula Röttger, Senden
Prof Peter Doyé, Technische Universität Braunschweig

Verlagsredaktion:
Claudia Schwarz

Zeichnungen:
Peter Stevenson (Linden Artists)
Jörg Plannerer

Projektleitung Grafik:
Beate Andler-Teufel

Desktop-Publishing:
(Typodata GmbH)
Sieglinde Milbradt
Viktoria Vogel
Heidi Höringer

Umschlaggestaltung:
Zero Grafik & Design GmbH

Der Inntenteil dieses Buches wurde auf chlorfrei gebleichtem Papier gedruckt.

1. Auflage

© 1997 Langenscheidt-Longman GmbH, München und Westermann Schulbuchverlag GmbH, Braunschweig

Das Werk und seine Teile sind urheberrechtlich geschützt. Jede Verwertung in anderen als den gesetzlich zugelassenen Fällen bedarf deshalb der vorherigen schriftlichen Einwilligung der Verlage.

Druck: westermann druck, Braunschweig
Printed in Germany
ISBN 3-14-25 0475-3

Hello, I'm Coco!

Und schon hast du deinen ersten englischen Satz gelesen!
Was meinst du, wie viele englische Wörter du sonst
noch kennst? Zehn, fünfzig, vielleicht sogar hundert?
Bestimmt weißt du schon mehr als du glaubst:
Denke nur mal an Wörter wie Jeans, CD,
Mountainbike, Skateboard, Popstar ... oder Clown!

Mich kennst du jetzt schon, ich werde dich durch
dein erstes Jahr Englisch begleiten. Aber auch
meine Freunde, die Mädchen **Kim, Madur, Pat** und
Rita und die Jungen **Alec, Grant, John** und **Mark**
werden dir immer wieder begegnen. Und du lernst
den alten Seemann **Len** kennen – mit seinem Hund
Skipper und **Mr Christian**, dem lustigen Affen.
Sie alle wohnen in oder bei Portsmouth, einer Stadt
an der Südküste Englands, die du auf der Karte
auf Seite XII findest. Schau' doch einfach mal auf die
nächste Seite, dort siehst du sie alle. In den *Units* erfährst du,
was die *kids* den ganzen Tag – in der Schule, zu Hause
in der Familie und mit Freunden in der Freizeit – so alles erleben.

Am Anfang des Buches, in der *Intro*, lernst du in kleinen
Schritten wichtige englische Redewendungen, die du immer
wieder gut gebrauchen kannst, wenn du dich mit
jemandem auf Englisch unterhalten willst.

Viel Spaß wirst du mit den beiden *Magazines* haben.
Dort findest du interessante Neuigkeiten über Bräuche
und Feste in englischsprachigen Ländern.
Außerdem geht es um Kino, Taschengeld,
Fernsehen und alles, was sonst noch *up to date* ist.
Wenn du Lust hast, kannst du sie alleine durchlesen oder auch gemeinsam mit deinem Lehrer
oder deiner Lehrerin besprechen.

Damit du im Unterricht selbst voll *in action* sein kannst, gibt es Partnerübungen ᴵᴵ und
Gruppenübungen ᴵᴵᴵ. Und immer wenn eine Aufgabe mit *Now you* beginnt ist dein Einsatz
gefragt.

Außerdem habe ich viele Lieder, Reime, Rätsel, Spiele, Bilder und Geschichten in diesem Buch
untergebracht, damit du noch mehr *fun* beim Englisch lernen hast.

Übrigens – alle Leute und Tiere kannst du auch auf der Textcassette 📼 hören und damit
sozusagen Englisch *live* erleben.

Ich wünsche dir viel Spaß und Erfolg dabei!

Dein Coco

CONTENTS

INTRO: New friends 1
English words 1

Step 1 1
Hello!
Alec und Pat treffen sich in der Schule.
− Sich begrüßen, sich vorstellen
  Hello./What's your name?/I'm ...

Step 2 2
Good morning
Drei Lehrer begegnen sich im Lehrerzimmer.
− Sich begrüßen, sich vorstellen
  Good morning./My name is .../Are you ...?

Step 3 3
Are you English?
Alec und Grant lernen sich im Klassenzimmer kennen.
− Sich begrüßen, sich vorstellen
  I'm ... And you?
  (Nationalitäten.)

Step 4 4
How are you?
Grant macht Rita und Alec miteinander bekannt.
− Jemanden vorstellen
  How are you?/I'm fine, thanks./This is ...
Song: Good morning

Step 5 5
Who's that?
Grant, Rita und Alec sprechen über ihre Lehrer.
− Jemanden beschreiben
  Who's that?/That's .../He's/She's .../
  He/She isn't .../okay, nice, ...
  (Namen.)

Step 6 6
What's that in English?
Kim und Alec unterhalten sich in der Deutschstunde.
− Jemanden auffordern, etwas zu tun
  Come in, please. /Sit down, please.
− Nach Gegenständen fragen und auch danach, wie sie in einer anderen Sprache heißen
  What's that?/What's that in English, please?
  (Möbel. Schulgegenstände.)

INTRO

Step 7 9
That's my friend
Mrs Harman holt Mark von der Schule ab.
− Persönliche Fürwörter
  I, you, he, she, it
− Besitzanzeigende Fürwörter
  my, your, his, her

Step 8 11
Sorry, dad!
Während Mr Ross und Alec den Möbelwagen ausladen, passiert ein Missgeschick.
− Nach Eigenschaften fragen
  Is he/she/it ...?/Yes, .../No, ...

Step 9 13
We're Scottish
Mr und Mrs Smith treffen ihre neuen schottischen Nachbarn auf einer Party.
− Nach persönlichen Daten fragen
  Are you ...?/Yes, we are./ No, we aren't.
− Persönliche Fürwörter
  we, you

Step 10 15
They're new here
Mrs Smith und Ramesh Patel unterhalten sich über die neuen Nachbarn.
− Personen beschreiben
  They're .../They aren't
− Kurzformen
  I'm .../You're .../They aren't .../ ...
− Fragen und Antworten mit Yes/No
  Are you English?/Yes, I am./Is he ...?/...

Tasks 17
Listening: A quiz
Act the scene: Jemanden kennen lernen

UNITS 1/2

CONTENTS

UNIT 1: In and around Portsmouth 18

This is Portsmouth 18

A 19

Bighead!
Grant und John besuchen Mark, der mit seiner Unterhaltungselektronik angibt.
(Konsumgüter.
Eigenschaftswörter. Zahlen 1 – 12.)

B/C 20/22
– Sagen und fragen, was jemand besitzt
  have got: I, you, we
– Besitzanzeigendes Fürwort
  our
– Geschlechtswort
  a – an, the
– Mehrzahl
  cassettes, cars

D 23

Classroom talk
Rhyme: One, two, three, four
Quiz: Have you got a ...?

Time for revision 24

Geschlechtswort: a – an
Persönliche Fürwörter: I – you – he – she – they
Besitzanzeigende Fürwörter: my – your – his – her – our
Hinweisende Fürwörter: this
Writing: Write about your family

UNIT 2: Our friend Len 26

A problem 26

A 26

Len Bignall
John und Grant sind mit dem Fahrrad unterwegs. Grant hat eine Panne. Len, ein älterer Herr, hilft ihnen.
(Tiere. Haushaltsgegenstände.)

B/C 28/31
– Sagen und fragen, was jemand besitzt
  have got: he, she, it
– Besitzanzeigende Fürwörter
  my, your, his, her, our, their
– Nach dem Alter fragen und darauf antworten
  How old are you?/I'm ...
  How old is he/she?/He's/She's ...
– Nach der Anzahl fragen
  How many ...?

D 32

Listening: Len at home
Song: What shall we do with the drunken sailor?
Reading: Our friend Len
Writing: A friend

Time for activities 34

Picture game: What's in the picture?
Game: Have you got a ... in your pocket?
Picture game: What's the difference?

CONTENTS

UNIT 3: Morning, afternoon and evening 35

What's the time? 36

A 36

Where's Madur?
Kim und John suchen Madur. Sie treffen sie im Park, wo sie einem verletzten Vogel hilft. Sie bringen den Vogel zu Len.
(Zukunft. Steigerung und Vergleich.)

B/C 38/41

– Die Uhrzeit
  What's the time?/It's ... o'clock./ It's half past ...
– Steigerung und Vergleich mit -er:
  bigger than.../smaller than ... *
– Fragewort *where*
  Where's ...?/Where are ...?
– Über die Zukunft reden
  I'll/He'll/She'll/It'll/We'll
– 's-Genitiv/of-Genitiv
  John's house/Paulsgrove is a part of Portsmouth.
– Sagen, was man tun kann oder darf
  Can you ...?/I can't ... *

D 42

Act the scene: Telefonieren
Song: London's burning
Listening: How's Sam?
Classroom talk

Time for activities 44

Picture game: Who has got what?
Game: Let's draw
Words: Find twelve English words
Game: Two together
Make a poster!
Make a Christmas card!
Song: We wish you a Merry Christmas

UNIT 3/4

UNIT 4: Sports and games 46

The sports centre 46

A 47

The judo club
Kim ist unterwegs in den Judoclub. Pat will mitgehen und fragt ihren Vater, ob sie darf. Aber Mr Miller ist dagegen.
(Sportarten.)

B/C 49/52

– Sagen und fragen, wo sich etwas befindet
  There's, there are, there isn't, there aren't/ Is there ...?/Are there ...?
– Sagen und fragen, wie gut man etwas kann
  good at, not bad at, all right at
– Verlaufsform der Gegenwart
  I'm/He's/She's ... ing/What are you doing?/ Are you/Is he/she ... doing? *
– Sagen und fragen, was man kann oder darf; Bitten mit *can*
  can – can't (cannot)

D 53

Listening: At the judo club
Speaking: Activities in Portsmouth and in your town
Task: A survey

Time for a story 54

The box of nuts

---

* Diesen Teil der Grammatik braucht ihr nur zu verstehen und noch nicht zu lernen.

MAGAZINE 1/UNIT 5

CONTENTS

Magazine 1 55

Cinema food? 55
Kinder erzählen, was sie am liebsten im Kino essen.
(Einflüsse der US-amerikanischen Kultur: Essgewohnheiten)

**Great ideas
for more pocket money** 56
Vorschläge wie du dir dein Taschengeld aufbessern kannst.
(Englische Währung. Tätigkeiten.)

Halloween 57
Fest in englischsprachigen Ländern (Großbritannien und USA) am letzten Tag im Oktober. Kinder basteln dort Laternen aus Kürbissen.
(Feste und Bräuche.)

Silly jokes 58
Englische Witze zum Weitererzählen

UNIT 5: Fun with friends 59
A robot's morning 59

A 60
The super robot
Mark will Kim und Pat den Roboter seines Vaters vorführen. Aber der Roboter hat ganz andere Vorstellungen.
(Zahlen 13–100.)

B/C 62/64
– Uhrzeit
  It's five/ten/a quarter/twenty/twenty-five past .../to ...
– Einfache Gegenwart
  He/She/It speaks .../Mark likes ...
– Persönliche Fürwörter als Objekt
  I'll visit him./Do you visit her?/He visits us.*
– Fragen, wann etwas stattfindet
  What time ...?

D 65
Reading/Writing: My friend
Classroom talk
Game: School quiz

Time for revision 67

Act the scene: Um Erlaubnis bitten
Personen beschreiben: Talk about Len's friends
Words: The magic square

VIII eight

CONTENTS

UNITS 6/7

UNIT 6: Friends and neighbours .. 68
British houses 68

A 69
Where's Len?
John und Alec fahren nach Portchester, um Len zu besuchen. Skipper läuft ihnen aufgeregt entgegen. Len selbst ist nirgends zu sehen. (Körperteile. Wochentage.)

B/C 71/74
– Einfache Gegenwart: regelmäßige Tätigkeiten
 sometimes, often, always, every afternoon, on Mondays
– Fragen und sagen, wem etwas gehört
 Whose dog is this?/This is Len's dog.
– Sagen, was man haben möchte
 I'd like … /We'd like …
– Mengenangaben
 A packet of tea, a bag of sugar, … *

D 75
Game: Bingo
Rhyme: Seven days

Time for activities 76
Poster game
Missing letters
Tongue twisters
Game: Teatime with Len

Unit 7: Shopping in Paulsgrove .. 78
British money 78

A 79
Our shop
Im *Paulsgrove Club Magazine* beschreibt Madur den Eckladen ihres Bruders Ramesh.
At the shop
John und Alec kaufen für Len bei Ramesh ein. (Geld. Nahrungsmittel. Getränke.)

B/C 81/83
– Einfache Gegenwart – alle Personen
 *I/You/We/They sell Asian food./
 He/She/It lives in a flat.*
– Einkaufen
 How much is that?/That's …

D 83
Reading: Picnic day for teddy bears
Listening: At the shops
Writing: Your shop
Act the scene: Beim Einkaufen

Time for activities 85
The four seasons and the months
Words: Make two lists (summer/winter)

nine IX

UNIT 8/MAGAZINE 2

CONTENTS

UNIT 8: The Paulsgrove Carnival 86

That's smart! 86

A 87

Carnival in Paulsgrove
Pat und Kim streiten sich über den Karnevalsumzug. Pat erklärt einem vorbeikommenden Photographen den Weg zum Grove Club.
(Kleidung. Farben.)

B/C 89/92

– Einfache Gegenwart:
  Fragen, Kurzantworten mit *do*
  Do I/you/we/they ...?/Does he/she/it ...?/
  Yes, I do./No, I don't./Yes, he does./
  No, he doesn't.
– Den Weg beschreiben
  *Can you tell me the way to ...?/Go down ... /
  Cross .../Turn right/left at .../It's on the
  right/left.*
– Das englische Alphabet; buchstabieren
– ing-Form als Hauptwort*
– likes/hates doing something*

D 93

Reading: A letter to grandma
Writing: A festival in your town
Listening: The big parade
Act the scene: Den Weg beschreiben

Time for activities 95

Reading: Funny rhymes
Tongue twisters
Speaking: Talk about the Patels and the Harmans
Words: What words go together?
Game: A secret message

MAGAZINE 2 98

Do you watch too much TV? 98
Teste dich selbst. Siehst du zu viel fern?
(Einflüsse der US-amerikanischen Kultur: Fernsehkonsum)

Come to the circus! 99
Anton, ein Junge aus dem Zirkus, erzählt wie sein Tag verläuft.
(Freizeit. Tagesablauf.)

Silly jokes 100
Englische Witze zum Weitererzählen

Your letters 101
Leserbriefe von Kindern
(Hobbies. Einzelne Aspekte des britischen Alltagslebens.)

x ten

CONTENTS

UNIT 9: People far and near 102

Scotland – the four seasons 102

A 103

The Scottish boy
Alec wird von zwei Mitarbeitern der Schülerzeitung interviewt.
(Schulfächer.)

B/C 104/108

– Einfache Gegenwart:
 Fragen mit Fragewörtern, Verneinung
 Where/What/When do/does ...?/
 ... don't/doesn't like ...
– Steigerung mit -est*
 big bigger biggest

D 108

Task: Alec's timetable
Task: An interview
Game: Who's who?

Time for a story 110

The clever crow
Gegenwart – Einfache Vergangenheit*

PLAY 112

The class play: Ghost hunters
Zwei Journalisten kommen in das Willis Hall Tourist Hotel, um Photos des Gespenstes für die Hotelbroschüre zu machen. Um Mitternacht sieht alles zuerst gut aus – aber dann läuft etwas schief.
Listening
Acting

UNIT 9/PLAY

Anhang 116

Zweites Suchbild von Seite 34 116
The Paulsgrove calendar – Teil B
(von Seite 101)

Wordfields 117
Zusammenstellung der wichtigsten Wort- und Sachfelder.

Grammar 120
Übersichtliche Zusammenstellung der Grammatik, die in diesem Buch durchgenommen wird.

Vocabulary 134
Zusammenstellung der englischen Wörter und Wendungen in der Reihenfolge der Units.

Dictionary 156
Zusammenstellung der englischen Wörter und Wendungen in alphabetischer Reihenfolge.

Numbers, letters, sounds 163

👥 Partnerübungen kannst du mit einem Mitschüler zusammen machen.

👥👥 Gruppenübungen kannst du gemeinsam mit mehreren Klassenkameraden bearbeiten.

👥 Kettenübungen werden von der ganzen Klasse gemeinsam gemacht. Du antwortest einem Klassenkameraden und stellst selbst eine weitere Frage an einen anderen Mitschüler.

🎧 Texte, Übungen und Songs mit diesem Symbol findest du (auch) auf der Textcassette.

○ Die Übungen mit dieser Kennung sind etwas schwieriger und können gegebenenfalls weggelassen werden.

eleven XI

New friends

Intro

English words

Ihr kennt sicher schon eine Menge englischer Wörter!
Hier sind einige, die im Deutschen oft verwendet werden.

Für welche Wörter gibt es auch einen deutschen Begriff?

Jetzt übt mit eurem Lehrer/eurer Lehrerin, wie man diese Wörter so ausspricht, wie Engländer sie aussprechen würden. Kennt ihr weitere englische Wörter?

Step 1

Hello!

Pat: Hello!
Alec: Hello. What's your name?
Pat: Pat. And what's your name?
Alec: I'm Alec.

Now you.
A: Hello!
B: Hello! What's your name?
A: I'm (Peter). And what's your name?
B: I'm (Silvia).

one 1

Intro

New friends

Step 2

Good morning

Mr Wilson: Good morning.
My name is George Wilson.
What's your name?
Miss Green: I'm Miss Green. Jane Green.
Mr Wilson: Hello, Jane.

Mr Wilson: Are you Ann Dean?
Mrs Dean: Yes, I am.
Mr Wilson: Hello.

1 *Now you.*

A: Good morning. My name is (Peter).
B: Good morning. My name is (Silvia).
C: Good morning. My name is ...
D: ...

2 *Now you.*

A: Good morning. My name is (Peter).
What's ...?
B: I'm (Silvia).
A: Hello.

3 *Now you.*

A: Are you (Silvia)?
B: Yes, I am.
A: Hello, (Silvia).

---

1 Jemanden begrüßen

Hello.	*Hallo.*
	Guten Tag.
Good morning.	*Guten Morgen.*

2 Fragen und sagen, wie jemand heißt

What's your name?	*Wie heißt du?*
	Wie heißen Sie?
I'm Silvia.	*Ich heiße Silvia.*
My name is Peter.	*Mein Name ist Peter.*
Are you Ann Dean?	*Bist du Ann Dean?*
	Sind Sie Ann Dean?
Yes, I am.	*Ja.*

➤ Grammar S. 121, 1a; S. 130, 3a; S. 131, 3d

3 Das ist im Englischen anders:

You = **du** und **Sie**
Your (name) = **dein** (Name), **Ihr** (Name)

➤ Grammar S. 127, 4a/4b

New friends — Intro

Step 3

Are you English?

Alec: Hello. I'm Alec.
Grant: Oh. My name is Grant.
Alec: Hello.
Grant: Are you English?
Alec: No, I'm not. I'm Scottish. And you? Are you English?
Grant: Yes, I am.

1 Ask and answer.

1 *A:* Are you Turkish?
   B: No, I'm not.
   A: Are you English?
   B: Yes, I am.

2 *A:* Are you Greek?
3 *A:* Are you German?
4 *A:* Are you Italian?
5 *A:* Are you English?
6 *A:* Are you American?
7 *A:* Are you Scottish?

3  Let's say it.

[əʊ]
1 Hell**o**, **o**h, n**o**.
2 Hell**o**, are you Grant?
3 N**o**, I'm not.
4 **Oh**. I'm Alec.
5 Hell**o**.

[dʒ]
1 **J**ane, **G**eorge, **G**erman.
2 **J**ane and **G**eorge.
3 **J**ane is English, Peter is **G**erman.

2 Now you.

A: Are you (English)?
B: Yes, I am.
   No, I'm not. I'm … And you?
A: I'm …

---

1 Fragen und sagen, welche Staatsangehörigkeit jemand hat

Are you English?	*Bist du Engländer(in)?*
	Sind Sie Engländer(in)?
I'm German.	*Ich bin Deutsche.*
	Ich bin Deutscher.
Yes, I am.	*Ja.*

➤ Grammar S. 130, 3a

2 Das ist im Englischen anders:

name (**N**ame), **m**orning (**M**orgen)   Hauptwörter werden klein geschrieben.

Yes, **I** am German.   Das Wort 'I' wird immer groß geschrieben.
     Die Staatsangehörigkeit wird auch groß geschrieben.

Intro

Step 4

New friends

How are you?

Alec: Hello, Grant, how are you?
Grant: I'm fine, thanks.
Alec, this is Rita, my sister.
Rita, this is Alec.
Alec: Hello.
Rita: Hello.

1  Now you.

A: How are you?
B: I'm fine, thanks.
C: How are you?
D: I'm ...

2 What are they saying?

1   A: Rita, this is John.
        John, this is Rita.
    B: Hello.
    C: Hello.

2   ...

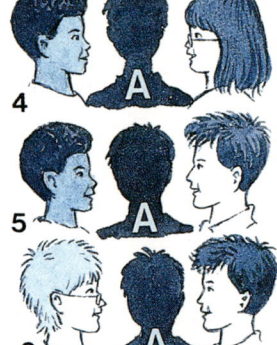

3  Now you.

A: (Silvia), this is (Peter).
    (Peter), this is (Silvia).
B: Hello.
C: Hello.

4  Now listen to the song and sing it.

---

1 Fragen und sagen, wie es einem geht

How are you?	Wie geht es dir?
	Wie geht es Ihnen?
I'm fine, thanks.	Mir geht es gut, danke.

2 Jemanden vorstellen

Alec, this is Rita.   Alec, das ist Rita.

▶ Grammar S. 128, 4c

4 four

New friends

Intro

Step 5

Who's that?

Grant: Who's that, Rita?
Rita: Mr Wilson. He's nice.
Alec: And who's that?
Rita: That's Mrs Dean. She's the English teacher. She's okay.
Alec: And who's that?
Rita: That's Miss Green, the German teacher. She isn't nice. And German is awful.
Alec: German isn't awful. German is nice.

1 Ask and answer.

A: Who's that?
B: That's ...

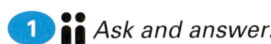

2 Ask and answer.
Look at the pictures in exercise 1.

A: Who's that?
B: That's ...

He's	nice.
She's	the German teacher.
	Scottish.
	okay.
	English.

3 Test your teacher!

4 Talk about the people.

He isn't ... He's ...
She isn't ... She's ...
He isn't English. He's Scottish.

1 Italian - Greek

2 German - Italian

3 English - German

4 American - English

5 Scottish - Turkish

6 Greek - Scottish

7 Turkish - American

5 Talk about the people.

Mr Wilson	is	okay.
Miss Green	isn't	nice.
Mrs Dean		

6 Talk about the people.

1 He's the English teacher.
2 She's the ... teacher.
3 ...

five 5

Intro

New friends

7 🔊 Let's say it.

[ð]
1 **Th**is, **th**at, **th**e.
2 Who's **th**at? Who's **th**is?
3 **Th**at's **th**e English teacher.
4 And **th**at's **th**e German teacher.

8 Words: please complete.

a - e - i - o - u

*ngl*sh   m*rn*ng   h*ll*   t**ch*r
G*rm*n   *wf*l   n*c*

1 Fragen und sagen, wer jemand ist

Who's that?   *Wer ist das?*
That's Pat.   *Das ist Pat.*

➤ Grammar S. 131, 3d; S. 128, 4c

2 He's/she's – he isn't/she isn't

He's English.   *Er ist Engländer.*
She's nice.   *Sie ist nett.*
He isn't English.   *Er ist kein Engländer.*
She isn't nice.   *Sie ist nicht nett.*

➤ Grammar S. 121, 1a; S. 129, 2a

3 The

The wird normalerweise [ðə] ausgesprochen.
She's the [ðə] German teacher.
Vor **a e i o u** wird es [ðɪ] ausgesprochen.
He's the [ðɪ] English teacher.

➤ Grammar S. 126, 2b

Step 6

What's that in English?

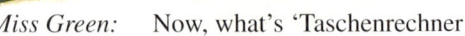

Miss Green:	Good morning, boys and girls.
Boys & girls:	Good morning, Miss Green.
Miss Green:	Come in, please.
	Now, sit down, please.
	Now, listen, please.
Kim:	I'm Kim. What's your name?
Alec:	Alec.
Kim:	Hello.
Alec:	Hello.
Miss Green:	Now, what's 'Taschenrechner' in English? Kim.
Kim:	It's a calculator.
Miss Green:	Yes.
Alec:	What's that in German, please?
Miss Green:	Kugelschreiber.
Alec:	Klugelschreiber.
Miss Green:	No. Ku - gel - schrei - ber.
Alec:	Kugelschreiber.
Miss Green:	That's right.
	Now, stand up, please.

Intro

New friends

1 *What are they saying?*

Come in, please. - Sit down, please.
- Listen, please. - Stand up, please.

2 *Now you.*

A: Stand up, please.
   Now, sit down, please.
B: Stand up, ...

3 *Ask and answer.*

1 A: What's that in English, please?
   B: It's a book.
2 ...

4 *Ask and answer.*

A: What's that?   B: It's ...
   Who's that?

Intro

New friends

5 *What are they saying?*

he - she - it

Jim: Who's that?
Ann: That's Andy.
Jim: ...'s okay.

Jim: Who's that?
Ann: That's Jane.
Jim: Oh, yes. ...'s nice!

Jim: What's that?
Ann: ...'s a chair.

6 *Now you. Look at your classroom and ask your teacher.*

A: What's (Lichtschalter) in English, please?
T: It's …
B: What's …

---

1 Fragen und sagen, wie etwas auf Englisch heißt

What's that in English, please?	*Wie heißt das auf Englisch?*
What's 'Buch' in English, please?	*Wie heißt 'Buch' auf Englisch?*
It's a book.	*Es heißt 'book'.*

▶ *Grammar S. 131, 3d*

2 Das ist im Englischen besonders wichtig:

Bei Bitten sagt man so gut wie immer **'please'**.
'Thanks' musst du immer sagen, wenn jemand etwas für dich tut.

Vergiss die beiden Wörter nicht, sonst könnten Engländer oder Amerikaner denken, dass du unfreundlich bist.

New friends

Intro

Step 7

That's my friend

Mark: That's my classroom, mum.
Mrs Harman: Is that your friend?
Mark: No. That's my German teacher.
Mrs Harman: She's a teacher! She's very small. What's her name?
Mark: Miss Green.
Mark: Look! That's my friend.
Mrs Harman: What's his name?
Mark: Grant.

1 *Ask and answer.*

1 A: What's his name?
   B: His name is ...
2 ...

5 A: What's her name?
   B: ... name is ...
6 ...

2 *What are they saying?*

my - your - his - her

1 What's ... name?
2 That's ... pen!
3 Look! George and ... sister.
4 What's ... name?
5 That's ... desk!
6 Is that ... bag, Jane?

nine 9

Intro

New friends

3 Ask and answer.

A: What's (his/her) name?
B: ... name is ...

Henry Alice Jane David John Mary

4 Now you. Test your partner.

A: What's his name?
What's her name?
B: That's (Peter).
A: That's right./That's wrong.

5 What are they saying?

I/my - he/his - she/her

I'm John and this is my team.

1 ...'m Grant and this is ...chair.
2 ...'m Mark and this is ...pen.
3 ...'s Andy and that's ... farm.
4 ...'s Mark and that's ... friend.
5 ...'s Kim and that's ... mum.
6 ...'s Jane and that's ... shop.

6 Let's say it.

[æ]
1 Pat, Andy, that, thanks, and.
2 That's Pat, that's Andy.
3 Thanks, Pat.
4 Thanks, Andy.

Intro

New friends

7 Words: make 2 lists.

Italian – pen – rubber – Scottish – blackboard – English – German – book

Turkish
Greek
...

chair
pencil
...

**1 Persönliche Fürwörter
(Personal Pronouns)**

I'm Grant.	**Ich** heiße Grant.
You're nice.	**Du** bist nett.
	Sie sind nett.
He's English.	**Er** ist Engländer.
She's okay.	**Sie** ist okay.
It's a rubber.	**Es** ist ein Radiergummi.

▶ Grammar S. 127, 4a

**2 Besitzanzeigende Fürwörter
(Possessive Pronouns)**

I'm Pat.	This is **my** book.
You're okay.	That's **your** bag.
He's nice.	That's **his** pencil.
She's Italian.	This is **her** chair.

▶ Grammar S. 127, 4b

Step 8

Sorry, dad!

Alec:	Oh, look, dad. That's Grant.
Mr Ross:	Is he your friend?
Alec:	Yes, he is. And that's Kim.
Alec:	Hello, Kim. Hello, Grant.
Kim & Grant:	Hello.
Grant:	Is that your house?
Alec:	Yes, it is.
Kim:	Is it nice?
Alec:	Yes, it is. It's big. That's my dad.
Kim:	What about your mum? Is she here?
Alec:	No, she isn't.
Alec:	Dad, this is Kim and this is Grant.
Mr Ross:	Hello. Oh no! Alec, you're awful!
Alec:	Sorry, dad.

eleven 11

Intro

New friends

1 Ask and answer.

1. A: That's Kim.
   B: Is she nice?
   A: Yes, she is.
2. A: ... Grant.
   B: Is ... English?
   A: Yes, he ...
3. A: ... my house.
   B: Is ... nice?
   A: Yes, it ...
4. A: ... my pen.
   B: Is ... good?
   A: Yes, it ...
5. A: ... Mrs Dean.
   B: Is ... okay?
   A: Yes, she ...
6. A: ... Alec.
   B: Is ... Scottish?
   A: Yes, he ...

3 Please answer.

| Yes, | he
she
it | is. | No, | he
she
it | isn't. |

Is she nice?
Yes, she is.

Is it big?

Is it small?

Is he awful?

Is she nice?

Is it small?

2 Ask and answer.

1. A: Is he English?
   B: No, he isn't.
2. A: Is ... American?
   B: No, she ...
3. A: Is ... Italian?
   B: No, she ...
4. A: Is ... German?
   B: No, he ...
5. A: Is ... Turkish?
   B: No, he ...
6. A: Is ... Greek?
   B: No, he ...
7. A: Is ... Scottish?
   B: No, she ...

4 What are they saying?

am - 'm - are - is - 's - isn't

Miss Green: ... you Alec Ross?
Alec: Yes, I ...
Miss Green: ... that your dad?
Alec: Yes, Miss.
Miss Green: ... you English?
Alec: No, I ... not.
Miss Green: ... your dad English?
Alec: No, he ... He ... Scottish.
Miss Green: And you? ... you Scottish?
Alec: Yes, I ...

New friends

Intro

5 🎧 *Let's say it.*

[ɔː]
1. Sm**a**ll, **aw**ful, m**or**ning, Ge**or**ge, y**our**.
2. A sm**a**ll **aw**ful boy.
3. Good m**or**ning, Ge**or**ge.
4. Oh, good m**or**ning. What's y**our** name?
5. I'm Ge**or**ge.

[ɜː]
1. G**ir**l, G**er**man.
2. G**er**man g**ir**l.
3. Sit down, g**ir**ls.
4. Come in, G**er**man g**ir**ls.

Step 9

We're Scottish

🎧
Mr Ross: Hello. We're Mr and Mrs Ross.
Mr Smith: Hello. My name is Orville Smith and this is Ruth.
Mrs Ross: Hello. My name is Alison.
Mr Ross: Yes, and I'm Stuart.
Mrs Smith: Hello. Are you new here?
Mrs Ross: Yes, we are. What about you?
Mrs Smith: Oh, no, we aren't new here.
Mr Smith: And are you English, Alison?
Mrs Ross: No, we aren't. We're Scottish.
Mrs Smith: Oh, you're Scottish? That's nice.
Mr Ross: And what about you? Are you English?
Mrs Smith: Yes, we are.

1 *What are they saying?*

I'm - We're

... German.
... American.
... Greek.
... English.
... Italian.
... Turkish.

thirteen 13

Intro

New friends

2 *Ask and answer.*

1. Smith - Ross
   A: Are you Mr and Mrs Smith?
   B: No, we aren't. We're Mr and Mrs Ross.
2. Miller - Ross
3. Roberts - Miller
4. Wilson - Dean
5. Ross - Roberts
6. Miller - Wilson

4 *Let's say it.*

[aʊ]

1. About, down, house, how, now, sounds.
2. Sounds, sounds, sounds.
3. Sit down now.
4. Now, how are you?
5. This is my house. What about your house?

3 *Ask and answer.*

A: Are you (Turkish)?
B: Yes, we are.
   No, we aren't. We're …

Persönliche Fürwörter (Personal Pronouns)

We're Mr and Mrs Ross.	*Wir sind Herr und Frau Ross.*
We aren't English.	*Wir sind keine Engländer.*
You're Scottish.	*Ihr seid Schotten.*
Are you Scottish?	Yes, **we are.**
Are you English?	No, **we aren't**.

➤ Grammar S. 121, 1a; S. 127, 4a; S. 130, 3a

New friends

Intro

Step 10

They're new here

Mrs Smith: Good morning, Stuart. Good morning, Alison.
Mr & Mrs Ross: Hello, Ruth.

Mrs Smith: That's Mr and Mrs Ross.
Ramesh Patel: Mr and Mrs Ross? Are they new here?
Mrs Smith: Yes, they are. They're Scottish.
Ramesh Patel: Oh, they aren't English. They're Scottish. That's nice.

1 Talk about the people.

1 They're Scottish.
2 ...

2 Ask and answer.

A: Are they ...?
B: Yes, they are.
   No, they aren't. They're ...

1 Mr and Mrs Smith - Scottish
   A: Are they Scottish?
   B: No, they aren't. They're English.

2 Grant and Rita - Scottish
3 Pat and John - English
4 Mr and Mrs Ross - English
5 Alec and Mr Ross - Scottish
6 Mark and Mrs Harman - American

3  Let's say it.

[uː]

1 Classr**oo**m, wh**o**, y**ou**.
2 Wh**o**'s that? That's y**ou**.
3 That's y**ou** and that's your classr**oo**m.
4 Wh**o**'s that? - That's y**ou**. - Wh**o**? - Y**ou**.

4 Words: Was sagst du, wenn ...

1 du dich entschuldigen willst?
2 du dich bedanken willst?
3 du um etwas bittest?
4 du fragen willst, wie es jemandem geht?
5 du antworten willst, dass es dir gut geht?
6 du wissen willst, wie etwas auf Englisch heißt?

a) Sorry.
b) What's that in English?
c) Thanks.
d) Please.
e) How are you?
f) Fine, thanks.

fifteen 15

Intro

New friends

5 *Classroom talk: what are they saying?*

Persönliche Fürwörter (Personal Pronouns)

They're Scottish.	*Sie sind Schotten.*
They aren't English.	*Sie sind keine Engländer.*
Are they new here?	Yes, **they are.**/No, **they aren't**.

➤ *Grammar S. 127, 4a*

2 Kurzformen (Short Forms)

Im Englischen werden **am are is** sehr häufig abgekürzt, besonders beim Sprechen.

Auch die Verneinung kannst du abkürzen.

Kurzform	Langform
I'm	I am
we're	we are
you're	you are
they're	they are
he's	he is
she's	she is
it's	it is
who's	who is
what's	what is

Kurzform	Langform
I'm not	I am not
we aren't	we are not
you aren't	you are not
they aren't	they are not
he isn't	he is not
she isn't	she is not
it isn't	it is not

Bei **Fragen und Antworten mit 'Yes/No'** benutzt man Kurzformen nur in der Antwort mit 'No':

Frage	Antwort mit Yes	Antwort mit No
Langform	**Langform**	**Kurzform**
Are you English?	Yes, I am.	No, I'm not.
Are you English?	Yes, we are.	No, we aren't.
Are we English?	Yes, you are.	No, you aren't.
Are they English?	Yes, they are.	No, they aren't.
Is he English?	Yes, he is.	No, he isn't.
Is she English?	Yes, she is.	No, she isn't.
Is it new?	Yes, it is.	No, it isn't.

➤ *Grammar S. 121, 1a*

Intro

New friends

1 A quiz

1 Listen to the cassette.

2 Right or wrong?

a) Coco is a professor.
b) It's a German quiz.
c) Coco is English.
d) Professor is a name.
e) The question is: What's that in German?
f) 'Chair' is right.
g) 'Hellophone' is right.
h) 'Telephone' is wrong.

Tasks

2 Act the scene

A: Begrüße B.

B: Begrüße A.
    Frage A, wie er/sie heißt.

A: Sage, wie du heißt.
    Frage B, wie er/sie heißt.

B: Sage, wie du heißt.
    Frage A, ob er/sie Engländer/in ist.

A: Sage, du bist kein/e Engländer/in.
    Sage, aus welchem Land du kommst.

B: Frage, wer das (das andere Mädchen) ist.

A: Sage, sie ist deine Freundin.

B: Sage, sie ist nett.

A: Stimme zu.

B: Frage, wie sie heißt.

A: Sage, wie sie heißt.

seventeen 17

UNIT 1   In and around Portsmouth

"The Victory"

This is Portsmouth

Portsmouth is a big British port.

Paulsgrove is a new part of Portsmouth.

This is Portchester
Portchester is an old town. It's near Portsmouth.

This is a house in West Street.

This is Castle Street in Portchester.

Portchester Castle

What's right?

Portsmouth	is	a	town near Portsmouth.
Paulsgrove		an	street in Portchester.
Portchester			big British port.
Castle Street			new part of Portsmouth.
West Street			old town.

18 eighteen

In and around Portsmouth

UNIT 1

A

Bighead!

Part 1

John: Hello. Is Mark at home, please? We're his friends.
Mrs Harman: Yes. Come in. He's in his room.

Part 2

Mark: Hello. Look, I've got a computer. It's new.
Grant: Wow! A computer!
John: Very nice.
Mark: Have you got a computer, John?
John: Yes, I have.
Mark: What about you, Grant? Have you got a computer?
Grant: No, I haven't.
Mark: I've got eight computer games. They're very good. This is a great game. Look.

Part 3

Mark: Look. This is our television. And we've got a great stereo. Have you got a stereo?
John: No, we haven't.
Mark: We've got a hundred video cassettes! Have you got a car?
John: Yes, we have. Our car is German.
Mark: We've got two cars.

Part 4

John & Grant: Goodbye, Mrs Harman.
Mrs Harman: Goodbye, boys.

John: Mark is a bighead! "I've got a computer and eight computer games."
Grant: "This is our television. We've got two cars." What a bighead!
John: Mark Bighead.

UNIT 1

In and around Portsmouth

A1 What's missing?

Mark: I've got a ...
I've got eight ...
John: I've got ...

A2 What's missing?

Mark: We've got ... and we've got a hundred ...
We've got two ...

A3 What's right?

John & Grant: 1 Mark is nice.
2 Mark is big.
3 Mark is a bighead.

A4 Can you say the numbers?

Numbers I

1 one	5 five	9 nine
2 two	6 six	10 ten
3 three	7 seven	11 eleven
4 four	8 eight	12 twelve

B

B1 What's right?

That's a/an ... car.
1 That's a British car.
2

B2 What are they saying?

1 I've got ...
2 ...

B3 Now you.

A: I've got a (computer).
B: I've got a ...
C: ...

B4 What are they saying?

Jane: Have you got a ... in your room?
George: Yes, I have./No, I haven't.

B5 Now you.

A: Have you got a ... in your room?
B: Yes, I have./No, I haven't.
What about you?
A: Yes, .../No, ...

chair   bag   pen
window   desk   pencil
computer   book   table ...

20 twenty

In and around Portsmouth

UNIT 1

B6 *What are they saying?*
1 We've got a house.
2 ...

B7 *Now you. Talk about your family.*

A: Have you got (a car)?
B: Yes, we have./No, we haven't.
What about you?
A: Yes, ... /No, ...

television   stereo   computer ...

B8 *Now you. Talk about your family.*

A: Have you got (a stereo)?
B: Yes, our ... is | new.
old.
big.
small.
nice.
okay.
awful.

B9 *What are they saying?*
big - great - nice - small - awful

1 What a ... book!
2 What ... game!
3 ... house!
4 ... an ... chair!
5 ... teacher!

B10 *Now you. Say the telephone numbers.*

one three five seven nine
two four six eight
five four three two one

A: What's your telephone number?
B: It's ... What's your telephone number?
C: It's ...

B11 *Words: what are they?*

a-e-i-o-u

1 Miss Green is the German t**ch*r.
2 Grant and John are fr**nds.
3 Grant and John are b*ys,
   Kim and Pat are g*rls.
4 Grant and John are *ngl*sh.
   What ab**t you?
5 We've got a G*rm*n car.

B12 *Words: two together.*

1 **big**   5 new
2 goodbye   6 please
3 hello   7 old
4 **small**   8 thanks

twenty-one 21

UNIT 1   In and around Portsmouth

B13 🎞 *Let's say it.*

[s]
1 Cassettes, books, desks.
2 Cassettes and books.
3 Books and desks.
4 Desks and books.
5 Desks, books, cassettes.

[tʃ]
1 Chair, Portchester, teacher.
2 He's a teacher in Portchester.
3 That's your chair, teacher.
4 One teacher, two teachers, three teachers.

[z]
1 Friends, games, cars, boys, girls.
2 Friends and games.
3 Friends and cars.
4 Boys and girls.
5 Girls and boys.
6 Girls, boys, cars, games, friends.

[aɪ]
1 Biro, fine, five, I've, nice, nine.
2 Four and five is nine.
3 I've got five nice biros.
4 Kim is nice. I'm fine.

C

1 A - an
I've got **a** new stereo.   I've got **an** old stereo.
Mark is **a** boy.   Mark is **an** English boy.

Vor **a - e - i - o - u** wird **a** zu **an**.

➤ *Grammar S. 126, 2a*

2 The
the = der, die, das

The boy is nice.   *Der* Junge ist nett.
The town is old.   *Die* Stadt ist alt.
The car is big.   *Das* Auto ist groß.

➤ *Grammar S. 126, 2b*

3 Mehrzahl
one car   two cars   *ein Auto   zwei Autos*
one book   two books   *ein Buch   zwei Bücher*

➤ *Grammar S. 125, 1a*

4 Sagen und fragen, was jemand besitzt: have got
I've got a television. (I have got)   *Ich habe einen Fernseher.*
We've got two cars.   (We have got)   *Wir haben zwei Autos.*
Have you got a stereo?   *Hast du eine Stereoanlage?*
                                            Habt ihr eine Stereoanlage?

Yes, **I have**.   No, **I haven't**.
Yes, **we have**.   No, **we haven't**.

➤ *Grammar S. 121, 1a*

In and around Portsmouth UNIT 1

D

D1 Classroom talk

Please read.

- Say that again, please.
- It's your turn.
- Say it in English, please.

D2 A rhyme

Say the rhyme.

One, two, three, four,
Come in, please, and close the door.
Five, six, seven, eight,
What's your name? You're very late.
Nine, ten, nine, ten,
Sorry, teacher, late again.

D3

Ask and answer.

Mark	John	Grant	Rita	Kim	Coco
car	car	book	stereo	computer	stereo
television	book	chair	pen	television	desk
chair	table	school bag	television	school bag	television
pen	house	stereo	biro	biro	biro
stereo	television	pen	desk	desk	telephone

A: Have you got ...?
Have you got ...?
...

B: Yes, I have.
No, I haven't.

A: You're (Grant).

B: That's wrong!

A: You're (Kim).

B: That's right!

Time for revision

1 What's right?

a - an

XXX: "My house is in Portchester. It's ... new house. Portchester is near Portsmouth. It's ... old town. I've got ... English stereo and ... American computer. My school is in Paulsgrove. Paulsgrove is ... new part of Portsmouth. We've got ... Scottish boy in our class."

Who is XXX ? Kim?
John?
...

2 What are they saying?

I - you - he - she - they

1 *Bill:* That's Jim. ...'s very nice.
2 *Stuart:* ...'m Stuart. Hello.
3 *Stuart:* Are ... Orville?
  Orville: Yes, ... am.
4 *Grant:* This is Rita. ...'s my sister.
5 *Ruth:* That's Mr and Mrs Ross. ...'re new here.

3 What are they saying?

my - your - his - her - our

1 *John:* That's ... dad.
  Grant: What's ... name?
  John: Bill. What about ... dad? What's ... name?
  Grant: ... name is Orville.
2 *Mark:* Who's that?
  Kim: She's ... friend.
  Mark: What's ... name?
  Kim: Pat.
3 *Grant:* Is that ... pen, Mark?
  Mark: No, it isn't. This is ... pen.
4 *Alec:* This is ... friend. ... name is Kim.
5 *Kim & Pat:* We're good friends. Miss Green is ... teacher.
6 *Mr & Mrs Smith:* ... name is Smith.

4 What are they saying?

this - that

1 *Miss Green:* ... is Alec Ross. He's Scottish.
2 *Mrs Harman:* Who's ...?
  Mark: ...'s our new teacher.
3 *Kim:* Alec, ... is Grant and ... is John. John, Grant, ... is Alec.
4 *Miss Green:* ... is your desk, Grant, and ...'s your desk, Alec.

Time for revision

5 *What's that in English?*

1 Wer ist das?
2 Sehr schön!
3 Uns geht's gut, danke.
4 Wiederhole das, bitte.
5 Wie heißt du?
6 Guten Morgen.

a) What's your name?
b) Say that again, please.
c) Good morning.
d) Who's that?
e) Very nice.
f) We're fine, thanks.

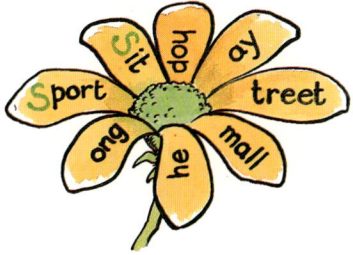

6 *Words: what are they?*

Sit, hop, ay, treet, mall, he, ong, Sport

7 *Write about your family.*

1 Hello. My name is Grant. I'm English.

2 My house is in Paulsgrove. Paulsgrove is a new part of Portsmouth. Our house is okay. Our telephone number is 63124.

3 This is my father. His name is Orville. This is my mother. Her name is Ruth.

4 This is Rita. She's my sister. She's awful.

5 This is my room. In my room I've got a chair, a desk and an old stereo.

Now you.

1 Take a piece of paper.
2 Stick photos of your family on it: your mother, your father, your brother, sister, cousin, aunt and uncle.
3 Stick photos of your house and room on it, too.
4 Now write about the photos.

UNIT 2

Our friend Len

A Problem

Speech bubbles: "This is great!" "Oh no!!!" "Have you got a pump?" "No."

Sign: ← PORTCHESTER

1 John and Grant are on their bikes.

2 They've got a problem.
   They haven't got a pump.

A

Len Bignall

Part 1

Len: Hey, you've got a flat tyre!
Grant: Yes, and we haven't got a pump.
Len: My name is Len Bignall.
Boys: Hello, Mr Bignall.
Len: Not Mr Bignall. I'm Len. What are your names?
Grant: I'm Grant and this is John.

Part 2

Len: Grant has got a problem.
      He hasn't got a pump, Skipper.

This is Skipper. She's got a pump.
Now, Skipper, get the pump, good dog!

Come in, boys.

→ A1

26 twenty-six

Our friend Len

UNIT 2

Part 3

Grant: You've got a monkey, too! What's his name, Len?
Len: This is Mr Christian.

John: Len, how old is Mr Christian?
Len: He's an old monkey. He's ten.
John: How old is Skipper?
Len: She's eight. How old are you?
John: I'm eleven. Grant is twelve.

Part 4

Len: Is it teatime, Mr Christian? Tea, boys?
John: Yes, please, Len.
Len: The cups are in the cupboard.
Grant: Oh, yes. How many, Len? Three?
Mr Christian: Eeek!
Grant: Sorry, Mr Christian. Is this your cup?

John: The milk and sugar are on the table.
Grant: Okay, now it's teatime.
Len: Good.

John: Len is nice.
Grant: Yes, and his pets are clever.

A1 *What's right?*

Len	has got	a pump.
Skipper	hasn't got	a flat tyre.
Grant		a problem.
John		

A2 *What's right?*

Len Bignall	is	a dog.
Mr Christian		a monkey.
Skipper		an old man.

twenty-seven 27

UNIT 2

Our friend Len

A3 *Please answer.*

1. How old is John?
2. What is Mr Christian?
3. How old is he?
4. What is Skipper?

A4 *What's right?*

Len	has got	the cups.
Mr Christian		the milk and sugar.
Grant		his cup.
John		the tea.

A5 *What's right?*

| The milk | is | in the cupboard. |
| The sugar | isn't | on the table. |

B

B1 *Talk about the people.*

they're - their

1. They're old. This is their house.
2. ... German. This is ... farm.
3. ... professors. This is ... book.
4. ... American. This is ... car.
5. ... nice. This is ... shop.

B2 *Talk about the people.*

A: Number one is Anne. She's got a desk.
B: Number two is Jim. He's got ...
C: ...

28 twenty-eight

Our friend Len

UNIT 2

B3 *Ask and answer.*

A: Has (Mark) got a ...?
B: Yes, he has./No, he hasn't.

A: Has Mrs Harman got ...?
B: Yes, she has./No, she hasn't.

	Mark	Mr Harman	Mrs Harman
computer	*		
television		*	*
car		*	*
desk	*		
stereo		*	*
bike	*		
house		*	*
handbag			*
shop		*	

B4 *Now you.*

A: I haven't got ...!
B: ...

book   computer   house   pen
car   dog   television   stereo   desk   bike   ...

B5 *What's right?*

1 (Grant) hasn't got a ..
2 ...

	Grant	Mark	Mr Christian	Len	John
computer		*			*
television				*	*
stereo	*				
pump		*		*	
cup	*		*		

B6 *Now you. Ask about the people in your class.*

A: Has (Silvia) got a ...?
B: Yes, she has./No, she hasn't.

C: Has (Peter) got ...?
D: Yes, he has./No, he hasn't.
E: ...

computer   telephone   sister
bike   dog   calculator   ...

twenty-nine 29

UNIT 2

Our friend Len

B7 What are they saying?

have - has

1. Grant: Mark ... got a computer. ... you got one, Kim?
   Kim: Yes, I ...
   Grant: Mark ... got eight computer games, too.
   Kim: ... he got a television, too?
   Grant: Yes, he ...

2. John: Len ... got two pets.
   Pat: Two pets? What are they?
   John: Len ... got a monkey and a dog.
   Pat: A monkey! Great! ... you got a pet, John?
   John: Yes, we ... We've got a dog, too.

B8 Ask and answer.

1. A: How old is Grant? B: He's twelve.
2. A: ... John? B: ...
3. A: ... Skipper? B: ...
4. A: ... Mr Christian? B: ...

B9 Now you.

A: How old are you?
B: I'm ... How old are you?
C: ...

B10 Ask and answer.

A: How many (books) has (Kim) got?
B: (She's) got (twelve books) and (a bike), too.

	Kim	Len	Grant	Pat	John	Ann
book	12					
cassette					11	
pen			8	6		7
bike	1					
desk				2		
chair		5	4		3	
cup		9				10

B11 English words?

1. neykom   4. limk
2. emattie   5. argus
3. bodarpuc   6. eta

B12 What are they saying?

at - in - on

1. Hello. I'm Grant. - Oh, yes. Come ...
2. John is not ... home.
3. We've got tea and sugar ... the cupboard.
4. The boys are ... their bikes.

B13 Let's say it.

[ʌ]

1. C**u**p, c**u**pboard, p**u**mp, r**u**bber.
2. **O**ne, c**o**me, n**u**mber, m**o**nkey.
3. C**u**ps in the c**u**pboard.
4. P**u**mps in the c**u**pboard.
5. C**o**me in, n**u**mber **o**ne.
6. N**u**mber **o**ne, m**o**nkey, c**o**me.

[v]

1. Clever, have, seven, eleven, Paulsgrove, television, very, video.
2. I'm clever, you're very clever.
3. We've got eleven televisions.
4. Oh, I've got seven clever videos.
5. Paulsgrove video club.

[iː]

1. Pl**ea**se, R**i**ta, sc**e**ne, str**ee**t, t**ea**, thr**ee**.
2. Act the sc**e**ne, pl**ea**se, t**ea**cher.
3. R**i**ta and P**e**ter and P**e**ter and R**i**ta.
4. A b**o**y in the str**ee**t.

Riddle

What is it?

A giraffe passing a window.

Our friend Len

UNIT 2

C

1 How old?

How old are you, John?	*Wie alt bist du, John?*
I'm eleven.	*Ich bin elf.*
How old is Skipper, Len?	*Wie alt ist Skipper, Len?*
She's eight.	*Sie ist acht.*

➤ *Grammar S. 131, 3d*

2 How many?

How many cups, John?	*Wie viele Tassen, John?*
Three.	*Drei.*
How many games have you got, Mark?	*Wie viele Spiele hast du, Mark?*
I've got eight games.	*Ich habe acht Spiele.*

➤ *Grammar S. 131, 3d*

3 Sagen und fragen, was jemand besitzt: have got

I've got (I have got) **You've got** (You have got) **We've got** (We have got) **They've got** (They have got)	a house.	**He's got** (He has got) **She's got** (She has got) **It's got** (It has got)	a house.
I haven't got (I have not got) **You haven't got** (You have not got) **We haven't got** (We have not got) **They haven't got** (They have not got)	a house.	**He hasn't got** (He has not got) **She hasn't got** (She has not got) **It hasn't got** (It has not got)	a house.

Have you got a house?	Yes, **I have**. / No, **I haven't**.
	Yes, **we have**. / No, **we haven't**.
Have they got a dog?	Yes, **they have**. / No, **they haven't**.
Has he got a friend?	Yes, **he has**. / No, **he hasn't**.
Has she got a bike?	Yes, **she has**. / No, **she hasn't**.

➤ *Grammar S. 121, 1a; S. 122, 1c; S. 129, 2b; S. 130, 3b*

4 Besitzanzeigende Fürwörter (Possessive Pronouns)

I haven't got a new pen.	**My** pen is old.
How are **you**?	Is this **your** friend?
He's got a problem.	**His** tyre is flat.
She hasn't got a problem.	It's **her** pump.
We are clever.	This is **our** new computer.
They are here.	This is **their** dog.

➤ *Grammar S. 127, 4b*

thirty-one 31

UNIT 2
D

Our friend Len

D1 🎞 **Len at home**

1 What's right?

Number one is …	a concertina. a fisherman. a ship in a bottle. a tin. a worm.

3 Now listen again.

a) How many cups have they got?
b) How many worms has Len got?
c) How many ships in bottles has Len got?

4 Now listen to the song and sing it.

What shall we do with the drunken sailor

What shall we do with the drunken sailor,
What shall we do with the drunken sailor,
What shall we do with the drunken sailor,
Early in the morning?

    Hooray and up she rises,
    Hooray and up she rises,
    Hooray and up she rises,
    Early in the morning.

Put him in the long boat till he's sober,
Put him in the long boat till he's sober,
Put him in the long boat till he's sober,
Early in the morning.

    Hooray …

(Traditional song)

2 Now listen to the cassette.

Has Len got	worms in a tin? sweets? a concertina?

drunken = *betrunken*
hooray = *Hurra*
long boat = *Beiboot*
sober = *nüchtern*

Our friend Len

UNIT 2

D2 **Paulsgrove club magazine**

Read the article.

Our friend Len

We've got a new friend. His name is Len. He's not in our class. His house is in Castle Street. That's in Portchester, not Paulsgrove. It's a very old house and Len is a very old man. Len has got two pets - a dog and a monkey! Skipper is his dog. The monkey is Mr Christian. Mr Christian is ten. Len has got great things in his house. He's got a concertina and six ships in bottles. And he's got worms in a tin - he's a fisherman. Len is an old fisherman. He's very old but very nice. And he's our new friend. Our new friend, Old Len.

John Roberts and Grant Smith

D3 **A friend**

Look at the article (D2) and write about a friend. Here's some help.

What's his/her name?
How old is he/she?
What things has he/she got? - Pets, stereo, ...

Time for activities

1 *What's in the picture? Write the words.*

2 *Play the game.*

Have you got a … in your pocket?

Yes, I have./No, I haven't.

3 *What's the difference?*

Hier und auf Seite 116 findet ihr zwei sehr ähnliche Bilder. Sie enthalten jedoch acht kleine Unterschiede, die ihr in Partnerarbeit herausfinden könnt. Einer von euch sieht das Bild auf dieser Seite an, der andere schlägt die Seite 116 auf. Fragt eueren Partner nach seinem Bild!

Have you got …? Is … in/on …?
Has … got …? I've got … in my picture. What about you?

34 thirty-four

Morning, afternoon and evening UNIT 3
What's the time?

1 Half past seven/Seven thirty

2 Eight o'clock

3 Nine o'clock

What's the time, please?
1 It's half past seven.
2 It's ...

4 Four o'clock

5 Half past five/Five thirty

thirty-five 35

UNIT 3
A

Morning, afternoon and evening

Where's Madur?

Part 1

Kim: Good afternoon, Ramesh. Is your shop closed?
Ramesh: No, it's open till eight o'clock in the evening. It's only half past five.
John: Is Madur here?
Ramesh: No, I can't find her. She's got a piano lesson at six o'clock.
Kim: Maybe she's in the park.
Ramesh: Can you look for her?
Kim: Yes, we can.
John: We'll find her, Ramesh.
Ramesh: Thank you.

→ A1

Part 2

Kim: There she is. Madur!
Madur: Hi, Kim! Hi, John!
John: What have you got there?
Madur: It's a seagull. It's hurt.
Kim: It's really big.
Madur: Look, its leg is broken.
John: Let's take it to my friend Len in Castle Street. He'll help.
Kim: Madur, you've got a piano lesson soon.
Madur: It's okay. My piano teacher's house is in Castle Street, too.
John: Okay, let's go together.

→ A2

36 thirty-six

Morning, afternoon and evening

UNIT 3

Part 3

Woman: Hello, Madur. That's a big bird. Is it a pet?
Madur: No, Mrs Johnson. Its leg is hurt.
Woman: Oh, dear. Will it be okay?
Madur: Maybe. We're on our way to our friend's house. He's got a lot of animals.

→ A3

Part 4

John: Len, this is Madur and this is Kim. They're my friends.
Madur /Kim: Hello.
Len: Hello, girls. What have you got there? It's bigger than Mr Christian!
Madur: Who?
Len: My monkey. He's smaller than this bird. Oh, yes, its leg is hurt.
Madur: Is it broken?
Len: No, no. But this bird is very tired and hungry.
Kim: Will it be okay?
Len: Yes, it will. I'll give it a fish and put it in the garden.
John: Will it stay there?
Len: No, it won't. It'll fly away soon.
Kim: Okay. Let's watch it.

→ A4

A1 *What's the time?*

It's	eight o'clock.
The lesson is at	five o'clock.
	six o'clock.
	half-past five.

A3 *What's right?*

| John, Kim and Madur are on their way to | school. |
| | their friend's house. |

A2 *What's right?*

The bird	is	broken.
The bird's leg		a big bird.
The seagull		a seagull.
It		hurt.

A4 *Please answer.*

Is Len's leg hurt? No, the ...
Who is smaller than the seagull? ...
What will Len give the seagull? ...

thirty-seven 37

UNIT 3

Morning, afternoon and evening

B

B1 *Ask and answer.*

1. A: What's the time, please?
   B: It's half past five.
2. A: What's ...?
   B: It's two o'clock.
3. A: ...?
   B: ...

B2 *Write the time.*

1. Half past six
   It's 6.30
2. Eight o'clock
   ...
3. Nine o'clock
4. Half past two
5. Five o'clock
6. Half past three
7. Half past four
8. One o'clock

B3 *What's right and what's wrong?*

How big is the seagull? The seagull is bigger than the monkey.   Yes, that's right.
How big is the monkey? The monkey is bigger than the seagull.   No, that's wrong.
Go on.

The pen is bigger than the pencil.
The cup is bigger than the cupboard.
The shop is smaller than the ship.
The boat is smaller than the bike.
The book is smaller than the blackboard.
The cassette is bigger than the castle.

Yes, that's right.
No, that's wrong.

1 pen / pencil    2 cup / cupboard    3 shop / ship
4 boat / bike    5 book / blackboard    6 cassette / castle 

B4 *Ask and answer.*

A: Where's the (monkey)?
B: He's (on) ...
   She's (in) ...

Morning, afternoon and evening

UNIT 3

B5 Ask and answer.

A: Where are the monkey and the bird?
B: They are on/in ...

B7 What's right?

fly away – give – help – put – take

1 *John/Kim/Madur:* We'll ... the bird to Len.
2 He'll ...
3 *Len:* I'll ... the bird in the garden.
4 I'll ... the bird a fish.
5 It'll ... soon.

B8 What's right?

1 That's Mr Harman's house.
2 That's ...

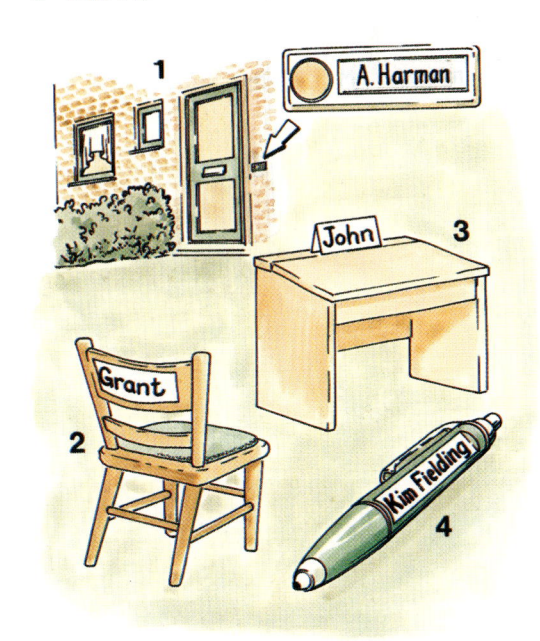

B6 Now you. Play the game.

1 A läßt seine Schulsachen im Klassenzimmer und geht hinaus.
2 Die anderen verstecken seine Bücher, Stifte etc. in oder auf dem Tisch.
3 A kommt zurück und fragt nach seinen Sachen:

A: Where's my (pen)?
   Is it in/on ...?
B: Yes, it is.
C: No, it isn't.
D: cold - warm - hot
E: …

UNIT 3

B9 *Now you. Play the game.*

1 A verlässt das Klassenzimmer.
2 Die Schulsachen von verschiedenen Mitschülern werden auf ein Pult gelegt.
3 A kommt zurück und versucht zu erfahren, wem die einzelnen Dinge gehören:

A: Is this (Silvia)'s (book)?
B: Yes, it's (Silvia)'s (book).
C: No, it isn't (Silvia)'s (book).
A: Is this ...?

B10 *Ask and answer.*

A: Is ... on his/her way to ...?
B: No, he isn't. He's on his way to ...
   No, she isn't. She's on her way to ...

1 Madur – John's house – Kim's house
   A: Is Madur on her way to John's house?
   B: No, she isn't. She's on her way to Kim's house.
2 Grant – Len's house – the club
3 Kim – Portsmouth – Portchester
4 Mark – the computer shop – the television shop
5 Madur – Grant's club – Kim's club
6 Alec – Portsmouth – the farm
7 Rita – the club – the film
8 Mr Christian – the film – the club

B11 *What are they saying?*

Grant: Come to my party, Len
Len: Who will be there?
Grant: ...'ll be there.

1 Pat   6 Kim
2 Alec   7 My mum
3 Madur   8 You
4 John   Len: Who, me? Okay,
5 Mark   thanks. I'll be there.

Morning, afternoon and evening

B12 *Talk about the pictures.*

What's the time? Is it open or closed?
It's (half past one/six o'clock). Number (one)/The (disco) is open/closed.

1 Swimming pool
  Open 9–5

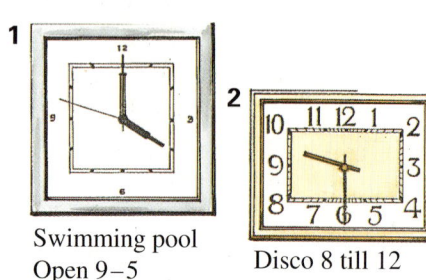

2 Disco 8 till 12

3 Video shop
  9–12 and 5–11

4 Portchester Castle
  9 to 6

5 Paulsgrove Club
  9 to 9

6 Windsor Piano
  School Open 9–4

B13 *Let's say it.*

[eɪ]

1 T**a**ke, pl**ay**, n**a**me, J**a**ne, g**a**me, t**a**ble, s**ay**, th**ey**, **ei**ght
2 Take the game, Jane. Play the game, Jane.
3 What's your name? – Jane.
4 They've got **eight** games.
5 The games are on the table.

[ɪə]

1 H**ere**, d**ear**, w**e're**, n**ear**.
2 Hello. W**e're** h**ere**.
3 Oh d**ear**! You're h**ere**.
4 Oh d**ear**! The monkey is n**ear**.
5 Is the monkey n**ear** h**ere**?

Morning, afternoon and evening

UNIT 3

c

1 Fragen und sagen, wie spät es ist

What's the time, please?	*Wie spät ist es, bitte?*
It's **one** o'clock.	*Es ist **ein** Uhr.*
It's **half past five**.	*Es ist **halb sechs**.*
It's **five thirty**.	*Es ist **fünf Uhr dreißig**.*

13:00   17:30

2 Anbieten, etwas zu tun.

We**'ll** look for Madur. *Wir suchen Madur.*
(We will)
I**'ll** give it a fish. *Ich gebe ihm einen Fisch.*
(I will)

➤ Grammar S. 124, 4

3 Fragen und sagen, was passieren wird (will-Future)

John**'ll** be at my party. *John wird auf meiner Fete sein.*
(John will)
He**'ll** help. *Er wird helfen.*
(He will)
It**'ll** fly away soon. *Sie wird bald wegfliegen.*
(It will)
Will it **be** all right? Yes, it **will**.
Will it **stay** there? No, it **won't**.
  (will not)

➤ Grammar S. 124, 4

4 's-Genitiv ('s-Genitive)

Len's house. *das Haus von Len/Lens Haus*
My teacher's house. *das Haus meines Lehrers/meiner Lehrerin*

➤ Grammar S. 125, 1b

5 of-Genitiv (of-Genitive)

Paulsgrove is a part **of** Portsmouth. *Paulsgrove ist ein Teil von Portsmouth.*

➤ Grammar S. 125, 1c

6 Steigerung auf -er (Comparative in -er)

Mr Christian is small. He's small**er than** this bird.
The bird is big. It's big**ger than** Mr Christian!

➤ Grammar S. 126, 3b

7 Fragen und sagen, was man kann oder darf (can)

I **can't** find Madur. *Ich kann Madur nicht finden.*
Can you look for her? *Könnt ihr / Kannst du sie suchen?*
Yes, we **can**. *Ja, wir können.*

➤ Grammar S. 121, 1a; S. 122, 1b

UNIT 3   Morning, afternoon and evening

D

D1 Act the scene

A:	Begrüße B. Frage B, ob seine/ihre Schwester zu Hause ist.
B:	Sage, sie ist nicht zu Hause.
A:	Frage B, ob sie gerade unterwegs zum Club ist.
B:	Sage ja, ist sie.
A:	Frage B, wie es ihm/ihr geht.
B:	Sage, dass es dir gut geht. Frage zurück.
A:	Sage, es geht dir auch gut. Frage wie spät es ist.
B:	Beantworte die Frage. Sage, du bist unterwegs zum Club. Verabschiede dich.
A:	Verabschiede dich.

D2 London's burning

Listen to the song and sing it.

LONDON'S BURNING (Traditional song)

London's burning,

London's burning,

Fetch the engines,

Fetch the engines,

Fire, fire,

Fire, fire,

Pour on water,

Pour on water.

engine = *hier: Feuerwehrwagen*
to pour on = *draufschütten*

Morning, afternoon and evening

UNIT 3

D3 How's Sam?

1 Listen to the cassette.
2 What's right: A or B?

A

B

D4 Classroom talk

Please read.

forty-three 43

Time for activities

1 Who has got what?

The monkey	has got a …,	a … and a …
The bird		
The dog		
The clown		
The professor		

2 Let's draw

head, eye, nose, mouth

Draw your partner. Show your drawing to your partner. Is it a good drawing?

Yes, but my	…	is	wrong.
		are	funny.
			awful.
			very big.
			very small.

Put your drawings on the wall. Who are all the people? Can you guess?

3 Find twelve English words!

BOTOJAKNAMLUGIRLOITUNTRISIONOMOVIBATOWNMOMALI
SOPENCILSOSOANOSUGARUIUIILOTILLABINPOESARARYBXN
MAARATARUARUSPASPORTONIPLEASEGUVEMOWINDOWEEM
TANKUWERYMUSHDOORAGWRITEOBIRDUIMWASHAGARETIYXRI
OLLOLLMONKEYASPLOSEHOMEYAPSTREETIGTENONEYOOTIVTZE

44 forty-four

Time for revision

4 *Game: two together.*

1. Macht euch das oben abgebildete Kartenspiel.
2. *A* hat die roten Karten, *B* die blauen.
   A legt eine Karte auf den Tisch,
   B legt eine Karte mit einem Wort dazu, das sich auf das Wort von *A* reimt.
3. Wenn das Wortpaar richtig ist, legt *B* eine neue Karte heraus, sonst bleibt *A* an der Reihe.
4. Wer zuerst keine Karten mehr hat, hat gewonnen.

5 *Make a poster!*

1. Look at German newspapers and magazines.
2. Find English words.
3. Make a poster.

6 *Let's make a Christmas card.*

1. Nimm ein festes weißes Papier und falte es in der Mitte.
2. Male etwas Weihnachtliches auf die erste Seite, z.B.:
   einen Weihnachtsbaum (a Christmas tree)
   den Weihnachtsmann (Father Christmas)
3. Auf die Innenseite kommt ein Weihnachts- oder Neujahrsgruß:
   Happy Christmas
   Merry Christmas
   Happy New Year
   A Merry Christmas and a Happy New Year
4. Nun fehlt noch die Anrede und dein eigener Name:
   To ... from ...

7 *Now listen to the song and sing it.*

We wish you a Merry Christmas,

We wish you a Merry Christmas,

We wish you a Merry Christmas,
and a Happy New Year.

A Christmas Carol

UNIT 4
The sports centre

Sports and games

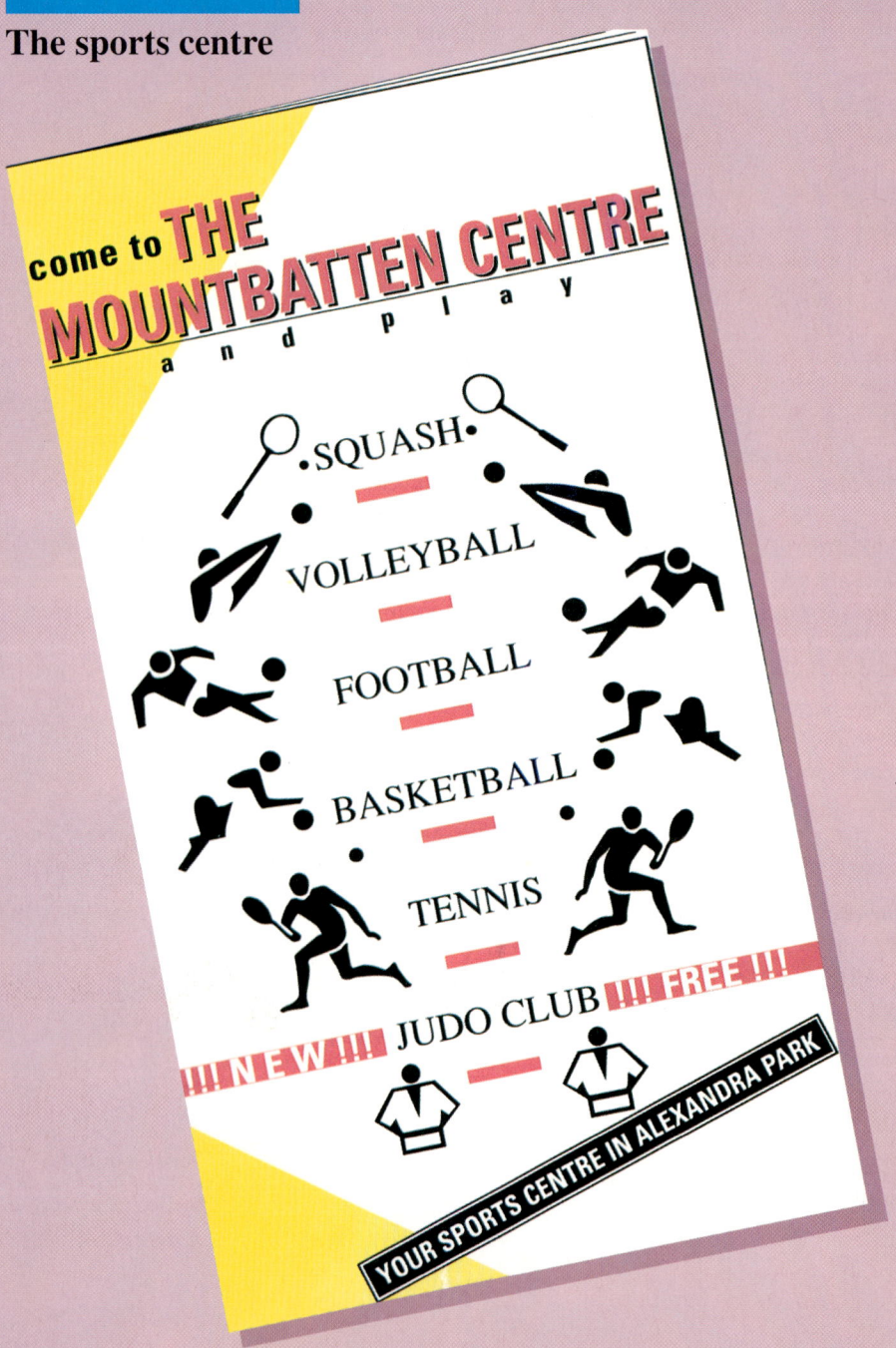

come to THE MOUNTBATTEN CENTRE and play

- SQUASH
- VOLLEYBALL
- FOOTBALL
- BASKETBALL
- TENNIS
- !!! NEW !!! JUDO CLUB !!! FREE !!!

YOUR SPORTS CENTRE IN ALEXANDRA PARK

What are the sports?

1 Number one is football.
2 Number two ...
3 ...

46 forty-six

Sports and games

UNIT 4

A

The judo club

Part 1

Pat: Hey, Kim! Where are you going?
Kim: I'm going to the judo club.
Pat: Judo? Is there a judo club here?
Kim: Yes, there is.
At the Mountbatten Centre.
Pat: Oh! That's new.
Alec: The Mountbatten Centre.
What's that?
Pat: A sports centre.
They've got volleyball and basketball.
Kim: And there's a squash club, too.
Alec: Squash! Great!
What about swimming?
Kim: There isn't a swimming pool.
Alec: What a pity!

→ **A1**

Part 2

Alec: Are you good at basketball, Kim?
Kim: I'm all right. What about you?
Alec: I'm not bad at it. I'm good at tennis.
Can you play tennis, too?
Kim: No, not really. But judo is fun.
Hey, Pat. Come to the judo club, too.
Pat: That's a good idea!
Let's ask my father.
Come with us, Alec.
Alec: I can't. Sorry.
I've got a lot of homework.

→ **A2**

UNIT 4

Sports and games

Part 3

Pat: Dad, there's a new judo club at the Mountbatten Centre. Kim is going now. Can I go, too?
Mr Miller: To a judo club? No, you can't, Pat. I'm sorry. Judo is for boys.
Pat: Oh, dad!

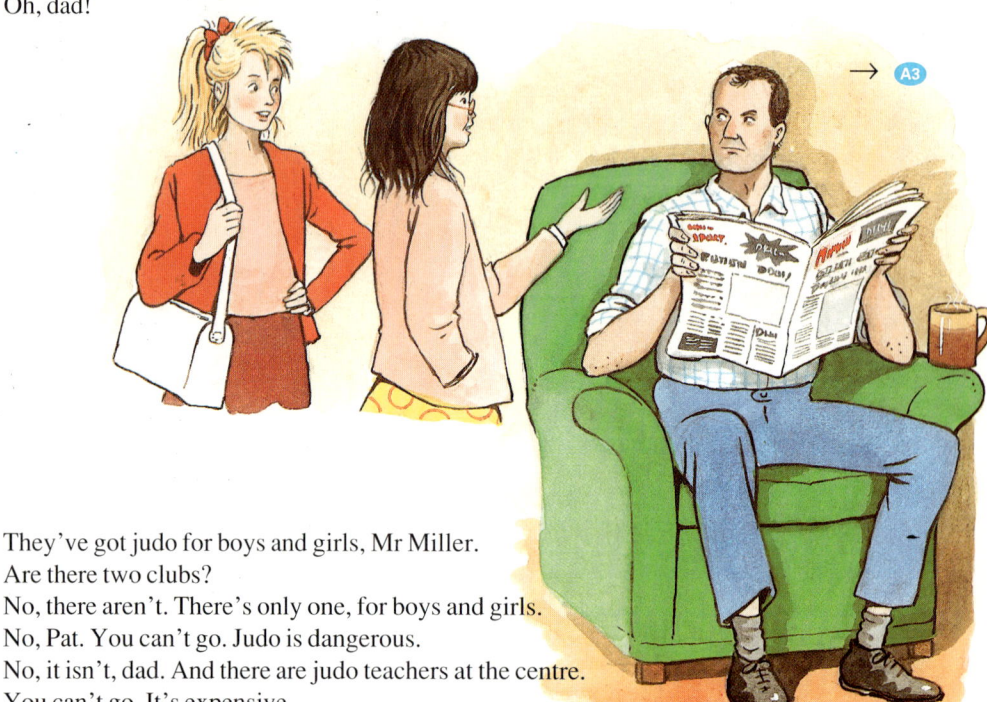

Part 4

Kim: They've got judo for boys and girls, Mr Miller.
Mr Miller: Are there two clubs?
Kim: No, there aren't. There's only one, for boys and girls.
Mr Miller: No, Pat. You can't go. Judo is dangerous.
Pat: No, it isn't, dad. And there are judo teachers at the centre.
Mr Miller: You can't go. It's expensive.
Kim: No, it isn't, Mr Miller. It's free.
Pat: Yes, and Kim can go. Oh, please, dad!
Kim: Yes, please, Mr Miller. Can Pat go, please?
Mr Miller: Well, all right, Pat. You can go.
Pat: Great! Thanks, dad! Come on, Kim.
Kim: Thank you, Mr Miller.

A1 What's right?

There's	a	swimming pool	at the sports
There isn't		squash club	centre.
		judo club	

A2 What's right?

Is	Alec	good at	basketball?	Yes, he is.
	Kim		tennis?	Not really.
				He's not bad.
				She's all right.

A3 What's missing?

Pat: Can I go to the ..., dad?
Mr Miller: No, you can't. ... is for ...
Pat: ...

A4 What's right?

There	is	two judo clubs.
	are	one judo club.
		an expensive judo club.
		a free judo club.
		judo teachers.

48 forty-eight

Sports and games

UNIT 4

B

B1 Ask and answer.

A: Is there a (squash) club at the sports centre?
B: Yes, there is.
   No, there isn't.

B2 Ask and answer.

A: Are there (four) TVs in the shop?
B: Yes, there are.
   No, there aren't. There are (three) TVs.

B3 Ask and answer.

1 Is there a table in the room?
2 Are there two chairs in the room?
3 ... a bird in the room?
4 ... three dogs in the room?
5 ... a television in the room?
6 ... two clocks in the room?
7 ... two school bags in the room?
8 ... a computer in the room?
9 ... a telephone in the room?
10 ... two beds in the room?

Yes, there is.   Yes, there are.
No, there isn't.   No, there aren't.

forty-nine 49

UNIT 4

Sports and games

B4 *What are they saying?*

1 There's a (monkey) in the old house.
2 There are ...
3 ...

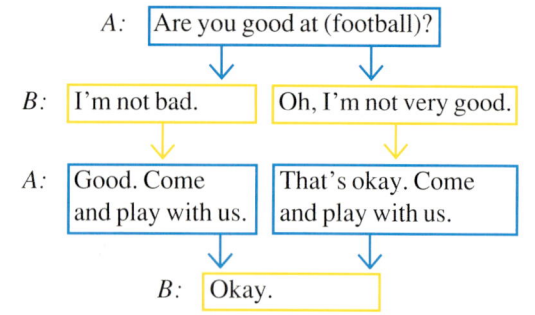

There's a ...
And there are ...

B5 *Now you.*

A: In our class there's (a blackboard).
B: In our class there are ...
C: ...

50 fifty

B6 *Now you.*

A: Are you good at (football)?
B: I'm not bad. / Oh, I'm not very good.
A: Good. Come and play with us. / That's okay. Come and play with us.
B: Okay.

football squash volleyball judo basketball ...

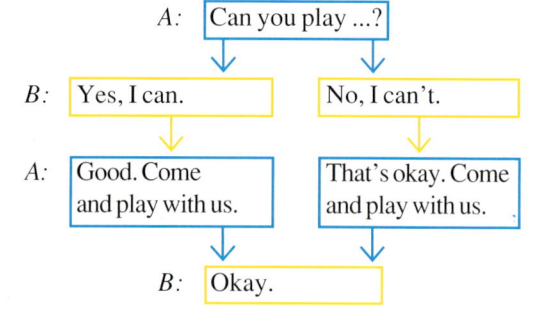

B7 *Now you.*

A: Can you play ...?
B: Yes, I can. / No, I can't.
A: Good. Come and play with us. / That's okay. Come and play with us.
B: Okay.

football squash tennis basketball volleyball ...

B8 *Now you.*

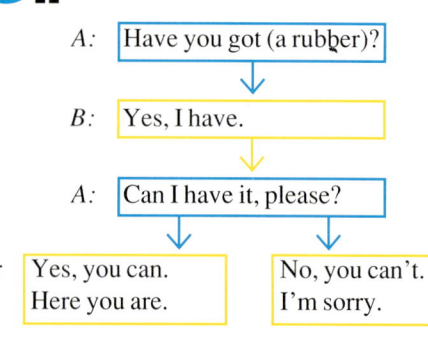

A: Have you got (a rubber)?
B: Yes, I have.
A: Can I have it, please?
B: Yes, you can. Here you are. / No, you can't. I'm sorry.

pencil biro rubber ...

Sports and games

UNIT 4

B9 Talk about Pat.

1. Pat can go to Kim's house.
2. Pat ...
3. ...
4. ...
5. Pat can't ...
6. Pat ...
7. ...

Yes, you can.
No, you can't.

1. go to Kim's house
2. watch the quiz
3. go to Alec's house
4. phone Kim
5. go to the judo club
6. listen to the stereo
7. watch TV

B10 Ask and answer.

1. Can you come to the club?

A: Can you come to the club?
B: Let's ask my mother.
B: Can I go to the club, mum?
C: Yes, you can. / No, you can't.
A: Well, can you come?
B: Yes, I can. / No, I can't.
A: Great! / What a pity!

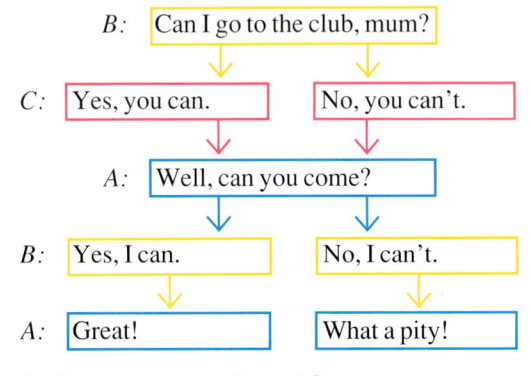

2. Can you come to the park?
3. Can you come to the sports centre?
4. Can you come to the football club?
5. Can you come to the swimming pool?
6. Can you come to the squash club?
7. Can you come to the judo club?

B11 Words: please complete.

at - for - to

1. *Kim:* Are you good ... tennis, Pat?
2. *Pat:* Dad, there's a new judo club ... the Mountbatten Centre.
3. *Pat:* Can I go ... the club, dad?
4. *Mr Miller:* Judo is ... boys.

B12 Let's say it.

[eə] Th**ere**, wh**ere**, ch**air**, th**eir**.
[ɑː] **Are**, c**ar**, b**a**sketball, Alex**a**ndra P**ar**k, f**a**ther.

1. Th**ere**'s a b**a**sketball club at the Mountbatten Centre.
2. Come and play volleyball and b**a**sketball. Wh**ere**? - At Alex**a**ndra P**ar**k.
3. Wh**ere are** the ch**air**s, f**a**ther? - Th**ere**.

[juː]

1. **You**, comp**u**ter, m**u**sic, **u**nit, **new**.
2. Are **you new** here?
3. Is that a **new u**nit?
4. Is that your **new** comp**u**ter?
5. Is that your comp**u**ter m**u**sic?

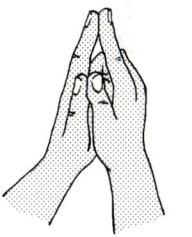

B13 Say the rhyme.

There's the church, There's the steeple,

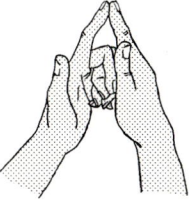

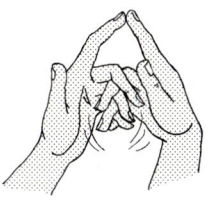

Open the door, And there are the people.

church = *Kirche*
steeple = *Kirchturm*

fifty-one 51

UNIT 4
C
Sports and games

1 There is – there are

There's (There is) a judo club at the sports centre.	*Es gibt einen Judoclub im Sportzentrum.*
There are good clubs at the sports centre.	*Es gibt gute Clubs im Sportzentrum.*
There isn't (There is not) a swimming pool.	*Es gibt kein Schwimmbecken.*
There aren't (There are not) two judo clubs.	*Es gibt keine zwei Judoclubs.*
Is there a squash club?	Yes, **there is**./No, **there isn't**.
Are there two football clubs?	Yes, **there are**./No, **there aren't**.

2 Sagen und fragen, wie gut man etwas kann

I'm **good at** tennis.	*Ich spiele gut Tennis.*
I'm **all right at** football.	*Ich spiele ganz gut Fußball.*
I'm **not bad at** judo.	*Ich bin nicht schlecht in Judo.*
Are you good at volleyball?	Yes, I am.
	No, I'm not.
	Not really.

3 Verlaufsform (Present Progressive)
Fragen und sagen, was jemand gerade tut.

Kim **is going** there now.	*Kim geht jetzt dort hin.*
Where **are** you **going**?	*Wo gehst du hin?*
Are you **going** to the club, too?	*Gehst du auch in den Club?*
Yes, I am./No, I'm not.	*Ja (, tue ich)./Nein (, tue ich nicht).*
What **are** you **doing**?	*Was machst du gerade?*
I'm doing my homework.	*Ich mache meine Hausaufgabe(n).*
I'm not going to the club.	*Ich gehe nicht in den Club.*

➤ *Grammar S. 123, 3*

4 Fragen und sagen, was man tun darf: can

Can I go to the judo club?	*Darf ich in den Judoclub gehen?*
Yes, **you can**.	
No, **you can't** (cannot)	

➤ *Grammar S. 130, 3b*

5 Um etwas bitten: can

Can I have your pencil, please?	*Kann ich bitte deinen Bleistift haben?*
Can you help me, please?	*Kannst du mir bitte helfen?*

➤ *Grammar S. 130, 3b*

6 What about?

What about swimming?	*Wie ist es mit Schwimmen?*
What about you?	*Und du?/Wie ist es mit dir?*

Sports and games

UNIT 4

D

D1 At the judo club

1 Listen to the cassette.

2 Please answer.

a) Where are Kim and Pat?   c) Is he good at judo?
b) What's the boy's name?   d) Is Kim good at judo?

D2 Activities in Portsmouth - activities in your town

1 What can you do at the Mountbatten Centre?

You can ...
There's a ...
There are ...
...

2 What can you do in your town?

I can go to ...
We can play ...
There's a ...
There are ...
...

D3 A survey

1 Here's a survey of the Paulsgrove people. Ask your partner questions about the survey.

A: Is (Pat) good at (squash)?
B: Yes, he/she is.
   He/She's not bad.
   Not really.

	Kim	Pat	Alec	Mark	Grant	John
Football	*	*	*	**	***	**
Basketball	*	***	***	***	**	**
Volleyball	***	***	***	***	***	*
Squash	*	*	*	*	**	***
Judo	***	**	**	*	***	**
Tennis	**	***	***	**	***	**

*** = good   ** = not bad   * = not very good

2 Now you. Make a survey of your group. Ask your partners and write the answers in a survey.

A: (Silvia), can you play (volleyball)?
B: Yes, I can./No, I can't.
A: Are you good at it?
B: ...

3 Look at your survey. Speak about your group. Start like this:

In my group there are (six) people.
(Two) are good at ...
(Silvia) is not bad at ...
...

fifty-three 53

Time for a story

The box of nuts

It's a nice summer day in the village of Crickwood. Mick, Pam and Dave, three hamsters, are sitting in a big tree near Joe's farm.

Mick: There are wonderful nuts in a box on the table in the kitchen.
Dave: Really? Nuts are nice!
Pam: Nuts are very nice! Let's get them.
Dave: What about the dog?
Mick: He's in the fields with Joe.
Pam: The problem is - how can we get into the kitchen?
Mick: Let me think. The key is always under the doormat. We can put the key in the lock. Then we can hang on it and open the door.
Pam: Great. Let's run.
Mick: Okay.
Dave: Let's go!

It's easy - and now the clever hamsters have got the nuts. They're going to the pond.

Pam: Let's eat the nuts under the tree near the pond.
Mick: That's a good idea!
Dave: Give me the box.

But the big box is full and very heavy.

Pam: Look! Dave is very tired. He's dropping the nuts in the grass.
Mick: Yes. Well, they're his nuts. Our nuts are in the box.

Now they're under the tree near the pond.

Dave: I'm tired and hungry. Let's eat the nuts now.
Pam: I'm sorry, Dave. The nuts in the box are for Mick and me. Your nuts are in the grass.
Dave: In the grass? Oh, no! Well, all right.

Pam: Very nice nuts.
Mick: Very, very nice nuts. What's Dave doing? Is he looking for his nuts?
Pam: I can't see him.
Mick: I can. Look!
Pam: Oh yes! Dave is in a nut tree. Look at all the nuts!
Mick: Yes, and look now. Here's Joe's dog. Quick! Run, Pam! Run!

MAGAZINE 1

Cinema food?

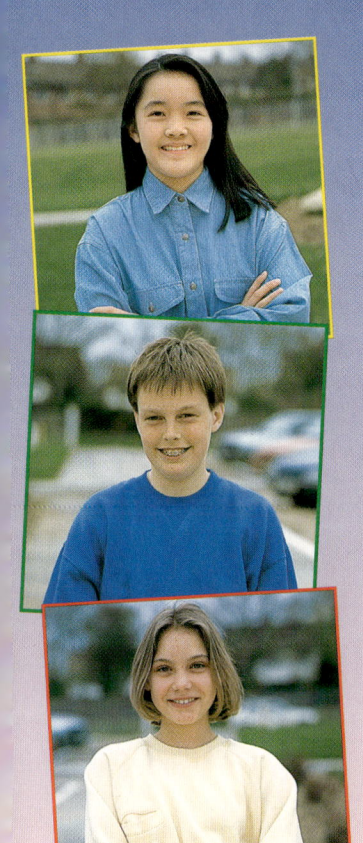

- My favourite food in the cinema is popcorn. I always buy a big bucket.

- I take a bag of sweets to the cinema. Sweets in the cinema are expensive and sweets from home are cheaper.

- At the kiosk in our cinema, the food is all American. There are hotdogs and hamburgers, ice cream and popcorn. Our bestseller is popcorn.

- I like cake and cola at birthday parties.

- My favourite food for breakfast? Cornflakes with cold milk!

What's your favourite food for the cinema, for breakfast, for a party?

apples   cake   crisps   hamburgers   ice cream   sweets

bananas   cornflakes   fries   hotdogs   popcorn

...	is	good	for ...	cinema
	isn't	my favourite food		breakfast
	are	okay		a party
	aren't	very good		

fifty-five 55

MAGAZINE 1

★★★ Great ideas for more pocket money ★★★

★ Have you got a grandmother or an old neighbour? Go shopping for her. Or clean her windows. She'll give you money for that.
★ Work in your garden or a neighbour's garden.
★ Baby-sit for a neighbour with a new baby or young children. Baby-sitting is easy money – the kids will be asleep a lot of the time and you can watch TV!
★ Visit an aunt or uncle on their birthdays and take them some flowers from your garden. Nice aunts and uncles will give you a pound.
★ Get breakfast for all the family on Sunday mornings for a month. After a month ask for more pocket money.

Have you got a new idea?

Ask your teacher for the words. Tell the class about your idea. Put all the ideas on the board.

What's (Autowaschen) in English, please?
And what's (Rasenmähen) in English?

MAGAZINE 1

Halloween

Halloween is on the last day in October, the evening before All Saints' Day. In Scotland and Wales people make fires on Halloween against ghosts and witches. In the United States, children have Halloween parties and go from house to house with Halloween lanterns and ask for sweets.

Have a Halloween party!

Invite your friends to your party. They can come as witches or Frankenstein's monster or Dracula.

Can you tell an American friend about a German custom like St Martin? (When? What? Why?)

fifty-seven 57

Magazine 1

Make a Halloween lantern.

1. Get a pumpkin.
2. Cut out the middle.
3. Cut out a face with eyes and a mouth.
4. Put a candle in the lantern.
5. Go from door to door, tell people about Halloween and ask for sweets.

Thanksgiving

In Europe we have our harvest festival in October. The first harvest by the British colonists in America was in 1621. In the USA, the harvest festival is called Thanksgiving Day. It is an American holiday. It is on the fourth Thursday in November.

Silly jokes

1
Boy: What has got four legs and can't walk?
Girl: Two pairs of jeans.

2
Boy: What have you got in your hands?
Girl: Guess.
Boy: Is it a mouse?
Girl: Guess again.
Boy: Is it an elephant?
Girl: What colour?

3
Girl: I can do what my teachers can't do.
Boy: What's that?
Girl: I can read my writing.

4
Boy: What are you doing?
Girl: I'm writing a letter to my friend Susie.
Boy: But you can't write.
Girl: That's okay. Susie can't read.

Fun with friends

UNIT 5

1 It's five to eight./ It's seven fifty-five. 7:55

2 It's ten past eight./ It's eight ten. 8:10

A robot's morning

What's the time?

a) The robot is at the breakfast table. It's ...
b) The robot is in bed. It's ...
c) The robot is on the bus to school. It's ...
d) The robot is at school. It's ...
e) The robot is in the classroom. It's ...
f) The robot is in the bathroom. It's ...

3 It's twenty-five to nine./ It's eight thirty-five. 8:35

4 It's a quarter to nine./ It's eight forty-five. 8:45

5 It's a quarter past nine./ It's nine fifteen. 9:15

6 It's twenty past nine./ It's nine twenty. 9:20

fifty-nine 59

UNIT 5
A

Fun with friends

The super robot

Part 1

Pat:	What's the time, Kim?
Kim:	It's ten to four.
Pat:	What time is the basketball club?
Kim:	It's at half past five.
Mark:	Listen. My father has got a robot.
Pat:	A robot?
Mark:	Yes, he's very clever.
Pat:	Clever?
Kim:	Oh, yes, he's very clever. He speaks French and German and ...
Pat:	Yes, and he lives at your house. And he sleeps in your room and ...
Mark:	Oh, shut up! He's at my dad's shop. Come and see.
Kim:	Okay, Mark.

Part 2

Mark:	Look! He can sit down. Robot, sit down!
Kim:	Wow! You're right.
Mark:	And he can stand up. Robot, stand up!
Pat:	He's great!
Mark:	Now listen to this! Robot, what's the time?
Robot:	It's a quarter past four. A cup of tea, please.
Kim:	He's right. The robot talks.
Mark:	He speaks French, too. Bonjour, robot.
Robot:	Bonjour.
Kim:	Ha, ha! This is super, Mark. What's his name?
Mark:	Robby Rob.
Mark:	Look! He walks, too. Robot, walk!
Pat:	Ha, ha!
Mark:	Help! Come here, robot!

Fun with friends

UNIT 5

Part 3

Robot: Fish and chips, please.
Man: Aargh!
Robot: Good afternoon. Can I dance with you, please?
Old lady: Oh, yes. Thank you. This is fun.
Pat: Look, Kim, he can dance, too!
Robot: You're nice.
Old lady: Thank you. And you're nice, too.
Kim: He likes her.
Pat: And she likes him.

A1 What's right?

Pat's	father	has got a robot	at home.
Mark's			at his shop.
Kim's			

A2 What's right?

The robot	can	sit down.
	can't	speak German.
		speak French.
		walk.

A3

the robot – happy – nice – the old lady

The robot is ...   The robot likes ...
The old lady is ...   The old lady likes ...

A4 What's the answer?

Who is in control of the robot?
– The man in the fish   – Mr Harman
  and chip shop   – Kim
– the old lady   – Pat
– Mark

A5 Can you say the numbers?

Numbers II

13 thirteen   21 twenty-one   31 thirty-one   40 forty
14 fourteen   22 twenty-two   32 thirty-two   50 fifty
15 fifteen   23 twenty-three   etc.   60 sixty
16 sixteen   24 twenty-four   70 seventy
17 seventeen   25 twenty-five   80 eighty
18 eighteen   26 twenty-six   90 ninety
19 nineteen   27 twenty-seven
20 twenty   28 twenty-eight
                     29 twenty-nine   100 a hundred
                     30 thirty   one hundred

UNIT 5

B

Fun with friends

B1 Ask and answer.

1 A: What's the time, please?
   B: It's five past ten./It's ten oh-five.
2 ...

1 10.05
2 9.20
3 4.15
4 6.45
5 1.10
6 3.45
7 11.30
8 8.25
9 7.15
10 2.35
11 6.55
12 5.40

B2 Now you. Ask and answer.

A: What time is your breakfast?
                     teatime?
                     class?
                     club?
                     ...?

B: (Breakfast) is at ...

B3 Talk about the people and pets.

eats - likes - lives - plays - speaks - walks

1 Alec Ross ... in Portsmouth.
2 John ... squash at the Mountbatten Centre.
3 Grant ... football.
4 The super robot ...
5 Mr Christian ... bananas.
6 The super robot ... English and French.

Riddle

What goes up when the rain comes down?

An umbrella.

B4 Talk about the people.

1
This is Mark Harman.
He lives in a big house.
He's got a stereo and a television.
He plays football.
He likes computer games.

2
- Alec Ross
- in Paulsgrove
- Scottish
- volleyball
- cars

3
- Kim Fielding
- in Paulsgrove
- small house
- judo club

4
- Len Bignall
- Portchester
- old house
- dog, monkey
- the dog's name
- the monkey's name
- tea

B5 Now you. Talk about a friend.

This is (Tanja).
(She) lives in ...
(She) likes ...
(She) plays ...
(She) ...

62 sixty-two

Fun with friends

UNIT 5

(Speech bubble: WHOO-HOO! IT'S TWENTY-TWO OH-TWO!)

B8 *Words: good or bad?*

an awful dog – a clever game – a great teacher – a dangerous sport – a happy class – a nice woman – a super stereo – a boring film

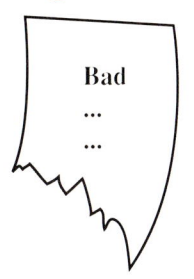

Good	Bad
...	...
...	...

B9 *Words: odd man out.*

1	2	3
come	listen	talk
listen	look	write
walk	watch	speak

B6 *How many are there?*

A: How many kids are there in our class?
B: There are twenty.

How many kids are there in our class?		
	boys?	in the classroom?
	girls?	
	shoes	
	teachers	
	windows	
	doors	

| There | is ... |
| | are ... |

B10 *Words: two together.*

1	**ask**	5	speak
2	come	6	write
3	give	7	**answer**
4	go	8	take

B11 *Let's say it.*

[w] **W**alk, **wh**at, **w**e, **wh**ere, **w**indow.
[r] **R**obot, f**r**iend, F**r**ench, ve**r**y, w**r**ite, **r**ight, g**r**eat.

1 Look! What a great robot!
2 Where are we going?
   We're walking to the club with the robot.
3 The robot is writing to a French friend.
4 Forget your pets, Len.
   We've got a great new robot here.

[ɔɪ]
1 This is a b**oy**.
2 This is a t**oy**.
3 This is a b**oy**'s t**oy**.
4 This is a t**oy** b**oy**.

B7 *Say the times*

A: What's the time, please?
B: It's eighteen minutes past seven./It's seven eighteen.

07:18
12:12
15:33
13:14
16:02
14:26
22:22

sixty-three 63

UNIT 5

Fun with friends

B12 *Say the rhyme.*

In the morning at eight o'clock,
Rat-tat-tat! The postman's knock.
Mary Carey opens the door,
One letter, two letters, three letters, four.
Two for mum and one for dad,
One for Mary, she is glad!

C

1 Die Uhrzeit (The time)

It's five minutes past eight./
It's eight oh-five. — 8:05

It's twenty minutes past eight./
It's eight twenty. — 8:20

It's twenty-five to nine./
It's eight thirty-five. — 8:35

It's a quarter past eight./
It's eight fifteen. — 8:15

It's half past eight./
It's eight thirty. — 8:30

It's a quarter to nine./
It's eight forty-five. — 8:45

It's ten to nine.
It's eight fifty. — 8:50

2 Einfache Gegenwart (Present Simple)
Sagen, was jemand immer, im Allgemeinen oder regelmäßig macht

The super robot **speaks** French.　　　　**He** speaks.　[-s]
The old lady often **dances** with the robot.　**She** dances.　[-ɪz]
The bird **lives** in a small house.　　　　　**It** lives.　　[-z]

➤ *Grammar S. 124, 3*

3 Persönliche Fürwörter (Personal Pronouns)

I'm ill. Please visit **me**.　　　　　　　*Ich bin krank. Bitte besuche mich.*
You're ill? Pat can visit **you**.　　　　　*Du bist krank? Pat kann dich besuchen.*
He's ill. John is visiting **him**.　　　　*Er ist krank. John besucht ihn.*
She's nice. Kim visits **her**.　　　　　*Sie ist nett. Kim besucht sie.*
We're ill. Please visit **us**.　　　　　　*Wir sind krank. Bitte besuche uns.*
You're ill, Kim and Pat?　　　　　　　*Ihr seid krank, Kim und Pat?*
　　Alec can visit **you**.　　　　　　　　　Alec kann euch besuchen.
They're ill. Grant is visiting **them**.　　*Sie sind krank. Grant besucht sie.*

➤ *Grammar S. 127, 4a, b*

4 Fragen, wann etwas stattfindet

What time is the basketball club?　　　*Um wieviel Uhr beginnt der Basketball-Club?*
It's **at** half past five.　　　　　　　　　*Er beginnt um halb sechs.*

Fun with friends

UNIT 5

D

D1 My friend

1 Read the letter.

Here's a letter from a reader:

My friend's name is Martin. He's eleven. He's got a big dog. The dog's name is Raffles.
Martin has got a good hobby - computers. He's got a small computer in his room! He plays football and he likes music, too. Martin is good at swimming. He hasn't got a dad at home. His mum is very nice. He's not bad at school.

George B.

2 Now write to the magazine about your friend.

How old is he/she?
Has he/she got a pet?
What are his/her hobbies?
Is he/she good at sports?

What has he/she got in his/her room?
Has he/she got a nice mum and dad?
Is he/she good at school?

UNIT 5

Fun with friends

D2 Classroom talk

Please read.

1 Can you do this exercise?
2 Can you help me, please?
3 Can I have your pen, please?
4 Can we do this together? Okay, let's work together.

D3 SCHOOL QUIZ

1 Make notes about a pupil or a teacher.

He/She lives in ...
He/She's ten/eleven/...
He/She plays ... and ...
He/She likes ... and ...
He/She is good at ... and ...
He/She's not bad at ...
He/She's got ...

2 Now tell the class about the person.

3 Now ask the class.

A: Who is it?
Class: Is it (Peter)?
A: No, it isn't.
Class: It's ...
A: Yes, that's right!

66 sixty-six

Time for revision

1 Act the scene

A: Schlage B vor, ins Schwimmbad zu gehen.

B: Sage, dass das eine gute Idee ist.

A: Frage C, ob er/sie auch mitkommen kann.

C: Schlage vor, deine Mutter zu fragen.

C: Frage D, ob du mitgehen darfst.

D: Sage, dass C mitgehen darf. | D: Sage, dass C nicht mitgehen darf.

B: Frage C, ob er/sie mitkommen darf.

C: Sage, dass du mitkommen darfst. | C: Sage, dass du nicht mitkommen darfst.

B: Drücke deine Freude aus. | B: Drücke dein Bedauern aus.

2 Talk about Len's friends.

1 John Roberts
   (Len/friend/Paulsgrove/good bike/squash)
   This is John Roberts. He's Len's friend.
   He lives in Paulsgrove. He's got a good bike
   and he likes squash.
2 Skipper
   (Len/dog/Portchester/sleeps on table/birds)
3 Mr Christian
   (Len/monkey/Castle Street/big cup/
   tea and bananas)

3 The magic square

How many words can you make?
1 come
2 nice
3 ...

N T O
A I M
R C E

UNIT 6   Friends and neighbours

BRITISH HOUSES

Now you. Talk about the houses.

1 The houses are (nice).
2 The house is …
3 …

Friends and neighbours

UNIT 6

A

Where's Len?

Part 1

Alec: Tell me about Len, John.
John: He's an old sailor.
Alec: An old sailor? How old?
John: He's sixty-eight. And he's got a monkey.
Alec: A monkey?
John: Yes, his name is Mr Christian.
They're always at home. Len works in his garden every afternoon.
Well, he does his shopping sometimes. And Mr Christian often helps him.
And Len goes to his club on Thursdays. Every week.

→ A1 A2

Part 2

Alec: Whose dog is that?
John: That's Skipper. Len's dog.
Hello, Skipper, girl. How are you?

John: Hey, what's the matter, Skipper?

Alec: Where's Len?
John: That's funny. He's always in the garden. Every afternoon.
Alec: Maybe he isn't at home today.
John: Oh, look, the door is open.

UNIT 6 Friends and neighbours

Part 3

John: What's the matter, Len?
Len: It's my leg, John.
John: Oh, is it bad?
Len: Yes, it's bad today, John. I can't walk. Hmmm, what day is it today?
John: It's Saturday.
Len: Oh, dear, oh, dear! It's my shopping day.
Alec: Well, can we do your shopping, Mr Bignall?
Len: Len. My name is Len.
Alec: Okay, Len.
John: Is that your shopping list?
Len: Yes, it is. Oh, all right. Thanks. Well, I'd like a packet of tea. A small jar of coffee. And I'd like two tins of dog food.
A bottle of milk.
Two boxes of matches
and a bag of sugar.
Oh, yes, and two bananas for Mr Christian.
Here's the shopping list, boys.

A1 What's right?

Len	has got	a monkey.
The monkey's name	is	sixty-eight.
		Mr Christian.

A2 Len Bignall's week. What's missing?

1 Len works ... every afternoon.
2 Len and Mr Christian are always ...
3 Len sometimes does ....
4 ... often helps ...
5 Len ... on Thursdays.

A3 What's right?

1 Where's Len today?
   a) He's in the garden.
   b) He's in his house.

2 What's the matter?
   a) Len's leg is bad.
   b) The door is open.

3 What day is it today?
   a) It's Thursday.
   b) It's Saturday.

4 On Saturdays Len
   a) does his shopping.
   b) goes to his club.

5 Len
   a) can do the shopping.
   b) can't walk today.

A4 Write Len's shopping list.

Friends and neighbours

UNIT 6

The parts of the body

Look at Mr Christian and learn the new words.

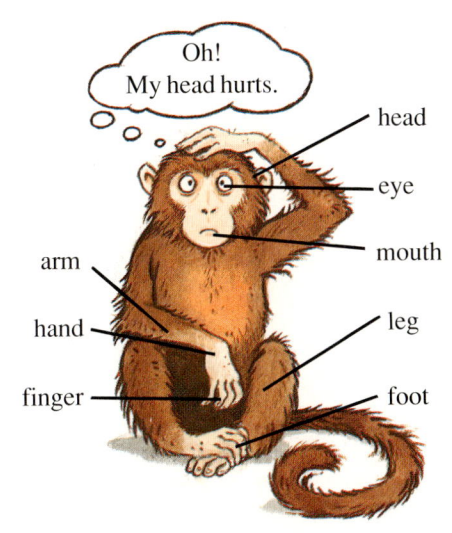

Oh! My head hurts.

- head
- eye
- mouth
- arm
- leg
- hand
- foot
- finger

A5 *Now you.*

A: Oh! My foot hurts!
B: Oh! My ... hurts!
C: ...

The days of the week

Can you say the days?

Die Wochentage werden im Englischen immer groß geschrieben.

B

B1 *Talk about the people.*

1 Kim goes on **Tuesdays** and **Fridays**.
2 Pat ...

Kim — **judo** and **basketball**
Pat — volleyball and basketball
Alec — volleyball
Mark — football
Grant — judo and football
John — squash

MOUNTBATTEN SPORTS CENTRE

Mon	Squash
Tues	Judo
Wed	Football
Thurs	Volleyball
Fri	Basketball
Sat	Squash
Sun	Football

Mon = Monday
Tues = Tuesday
Wed = Wednesday
Thurs = Thursday

Fri = Friday
Sat = Saturday
Sun = Sunday

seventy-one 71

UNIT 6

Friends and neighbours

B2 *Talk about the people. It's Saturday.*

1. John **sometimes** does the shopping.
2. He **often** watches television and goes ...
3. He **always** ...
4. Len ...
5. He ...
6. ...
7. Kim ...
8. She ...
9. ...

	do the shopping	work in the garden	watch television	go swimming	play squash
John	*		**	**	***
Len	**	***	*		
Kim	***	*	**	**	

*** = always   ** = often   * = sometimes

B3 *Now you. Talk about your mother and father.*

My mother My father He She	often always sometimes	does the shopping goes to town watches television plays ... works in the garden works at home phones friends	on Saturdays.

B4 *Talk about Fuzzy.*

dances - does the shopping - goes swimming - sleeps

1. Fuzzy ... every Tuesday.
2. He ... every ...
3. He ...
4. ...

Tuesday

morning

afternoon

evening

Friends and neighbours

UNIT 6

B5 *Now you. Talk about your mother and father.*

My mother	watches television	every	morning.
My father	goes swimming		afternoon.
He	does the shopping		day.
She	...		

B6 *Ask and answer.*

1 Whose monkey is that?
It's Len's monkey.

2 Whose house is that?
It's ... house.

3 ... mother ...?
...

4 ... bird ...?
...

5 ... sister ...?
...

6 ... house ...?
...

7 ... computer ...?
...

8 ... cup ...?
...

B7 *What is she saying?*

Mrs Harman:

I'd like	a	bag(s)	of	coffee.
	two	bottle(s)		dog food.
	...	box(es)		matches.
		jar(s)		milk.
		packet(s)		sugar.
		tin(s)		tea.

B8 *What's the number?*

42 1 **Forty-two**
    2 Twenty-four

27 1 Seventy-two
    2 Twenty-seven

38 1 Eighty-three
    2 Thirty-eight

69 1 Ninety-six
    2 Sixty-nine

76 1 Seventy-six
    2 Sixty-seven

83 1 Eighty-three
    2 Thirty-eight

54 1 Forty-five
    2 Fifty-four

95 1 Fifty-nine
    2 Ninety-five

B9 *Words: odd man out.*

1	2	3
boy	chair	basketball
dog	cup	judo
girl	desk	squash
man	table	tennis

seventy-three 73

UNIT 6

Friends and neighbours

B10 *Let's say it.*

[uː] Afternoon, who, you, two, do, food.
[æ] Man, matter, Saturday, packet, bag.

1 Good afternoon. Who are you two?
2 What's the matter, Len? Is it Saturday?
3 We can do Len's shopping on Saturday afternoon.
4 I'd like two packets of tea and a bag of sugar.

[f] or [v]?

1 Len's foot is very bad.
2 That's funny. My finger is very bad, too.
3 Football is very good fun.
4 Volleyball is very good fun, too.

C

1 Fragen und sagen, wem etwas gehört

Whose dog is this?   *Wessen Hund ist das?/Wem gehört dieser Hund?*
This is Len**'s** dog.   *Das ist Lens Hund.*

2 Sagen, was man haben möchte

I'd like a small packet of tea, please.   *Ich möchte bitte ein Päckchen Tee.*
We'd like two tins of dog food, please.   *Wir möchten bitte zwei Dosen Hundefutter.*

I'd like two bananas, please.   = *Ich möchte bitte zwei Bananen.*

3 Sagen, wie oft jemand etwas macht

a) Len **works** in his garden **every afternoon**.   *Len arbeitet jeden Nachmittag in seinem Garten.*
    every afternoon   *jeden Nachmittag*
    every day   *jeden Tag*
    every morning   *jeden Morgen*
    every Thursday   *jeden Donnerstag*
b) Len **sometimes does** his shopping.   *Len geht manchmal einkaufen.*
    Kim **often watches** television.   *Kim sieht oft fern.*
    John **always plays** squash.   *John spielt immer Squash.*
c) Grant and John **are often** at Len's house.   *Grant und John sind oft bei Len.*
    Len **is always** in the garden.   *Len ist immer im Garten.*

▶ *Grammar S. 132, 4b*

4 Sagen, dass jemand etwas regelmäßig an einem bestimmten Tag macht

Len **goes** to his club **on Thursdays**.   *Donnerstags geht Len in seinen Club.*

▶ *Grammar S. 132, 4c*

5 Aussprache -es

do	–	do**es**	[dʌz]	one box	– two box**es**	[–ɪz]
go	–	go**es**	[gəʊz]	one match	– two match**es**	[–ɪz]
watch	–	watch**es**	[–ɪz]	one hobby	– two hobb**ies**	[–ɪz]

▶ *Grammar S. 123, 2*

Friends and neighbours

UNIT 6
D

D1 Bingo

1 Mache dir eine Bingokarte.
2 Dein Lehrer oder ein Mitschüler ruft Zahlen aus.
3 Wenn du eine Zahl hörst, die du auf deiner Karte hast, kreuze sie an.
4 Hast du Kreuze auf allen Zahlen einer Reihe, rufe Bingo.
5 Wer als erster Bingo ruft, hat gewonnen.

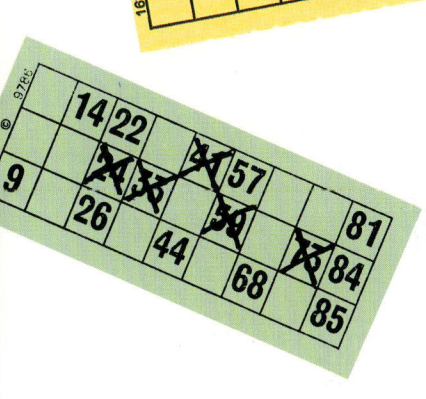

D2 Seven days

Say the rhyme.

Monday, Monday,
One day after Sunday,
Monday is our washing day,
There isn't time for games today.

Tuesday, Tuesday,
Our one–and–one–is–two day,
A lot of work at school today,
A lot of homework we can't play.

Wednesday, Wednesday,
Wednesday is friends' day,
You can come with us and play,
Everybody's here today.

Thursday, Thursday,
Maybe there's a birthday,
Party, presents, cake and then,
Oh, no! It's time for bed again.

Friday, Friday,
Fish and chips for tea today,
No more work till Monday,
It's a very happy day!

Saturday, Saturday,
Where's the list? It's shopping day.
Bananas, apples, biscuits, tea,
And milk and bread to buy today.

Sunday, Sunday,
Hobbies, sport and fun day,
And it's only one day till
Monday, Monday...

seventy-five 75

Time for activities

1 *Play the poster game.*

1. Nimm eine Zeitschrift und suche Bilder von zehn Gegenständen, von denen du den englischen Namen kennst (car, house, bike, book, computer, television, etc).

2. Schneide diese Bilder aus und klebe sie auf ein großes Papier. So erhältst du ein Poster.

3. Zeige dein Poster einem Mitschüler für ca. eine halbe Minute.

4. Der Mitschüler versucht danach, alle Dinge aufzuschreiben (natürlich auf Englisch!), die er auf deinem Poster gesehen hat.

5. Hat er alle zehn Gegenstände auf seiner Liste, gewinnt er; sonst bist du der Sieger.

2 *Find the missing letters.*

1. Suche dir zwei Partner.

2. Jeder von euch denkt sich fünf englische Wörter aus und schreibt sie auf einen Zettel. Setzt dabei an die Stelle eines jeden Selbstlautes ein Sternchen. Das Wort „football" würde z.B. so aussehen: f * * tb * ll.

3. Tauscht nun eure Zettel aus. Derjenige, der als erster die fünf Wörter errät, hat gewonnen.

3 *Can you say the tongue-twisters?*

She sells sea shells on the sea shore.

Pat placed Peter's parcel in the post van.

tongue-twister	=	*Zungenbrecher*
shells	=	*Muscheln*
shore	=	*Strand, Ufer*
placed	=	*legte*
parcel	=	*Päckchen*
post van	=	*Postwagen*

Time for activities

4 *Play the game:* **Teatime with Len**

Have you got a pawn and a dice ? Play with one to three partners.
You can say: What have you got? It's your turn. Come on. I've got a '1'! It's my turn. I'm the winner!

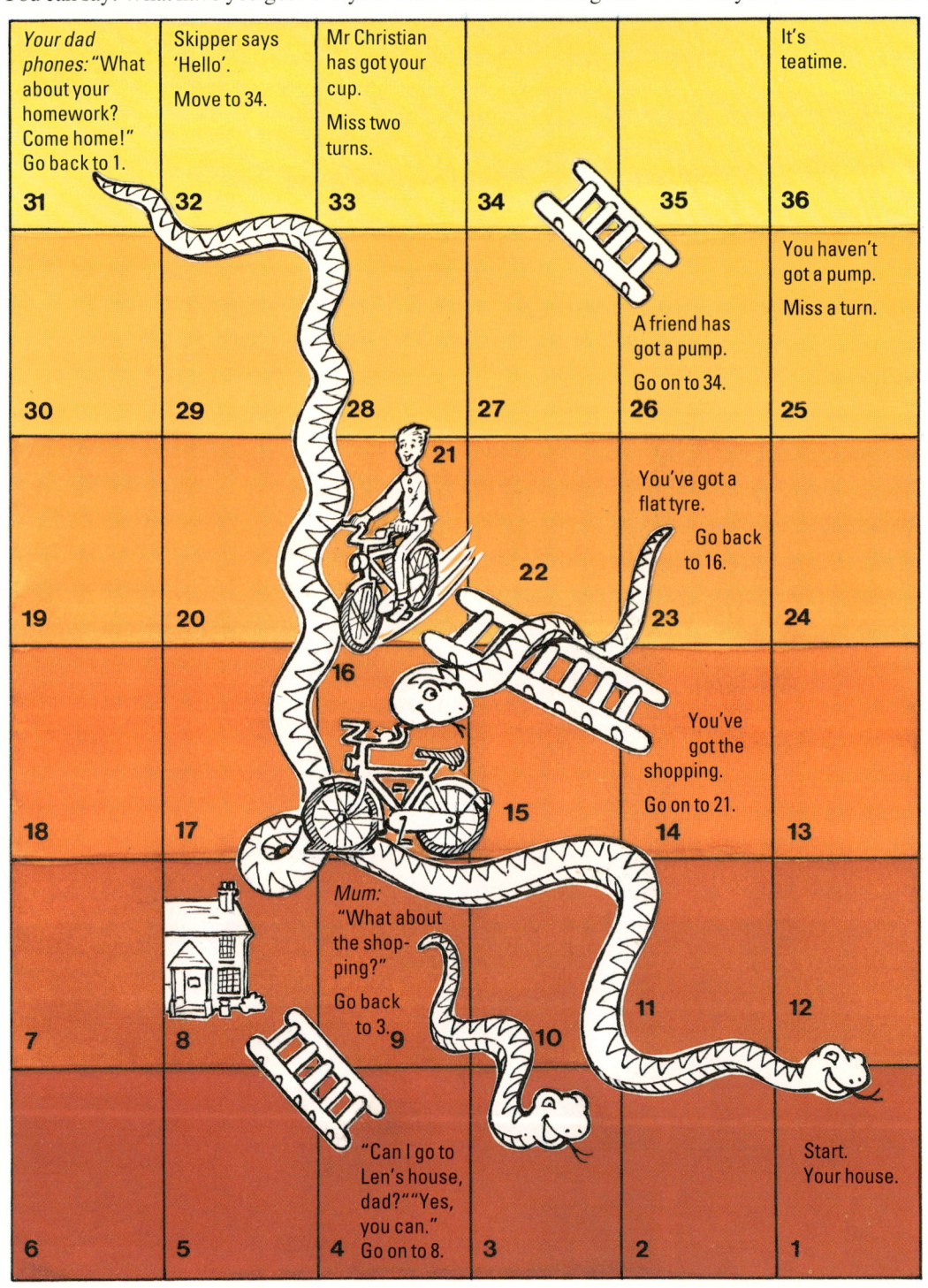

31 *Your dad phones:* "What about your homework? Come home!" Go back to 1.	32 Skipper says 'Hello'. Move to 34.	33 Mr Christian has got your cup. Miss two turns.	34	35	36 It's teatime.
30	29	28	27	26 A friend has got a pump. Go on to 34.	25 You haven't got a pump. Miss a turn.
19	20	21	22	23 You've got a flat tyre. Go back to 16.	24
18	17	16	15	14 You've got the shopping. Go on to 21.	13
7	8	9 *Mum:* "What about the shopping?" Go back to 3.	10	11	12
6	5	4 "Can I go to Len's house, dad?" "Yes, you can." Go on to 8.	3	2	1 Start. Your house.

seventy-seven 77

UNIT 7   Shopping in Paulsgrove

British money

Coins

Two pounds (£2)

Ten pence (10p)

One pound (£1)

Five pence (5p)

Fifty pence (50p)

Two pence (2p)

Twenty pence (20p)

One penny (1p)

Bank notes

Five pounds (£5)

Twenty pounds (£20)

Fifty pounds (£50)

Ten pounds (£10)

How much is that? Ask and answer.

A: How much is number (one)?
B: That's ...

£4.32 = four pounds thirty-two/four thirty-two
32p = thirty-two p [pi:]/thirty-two pence [pens]

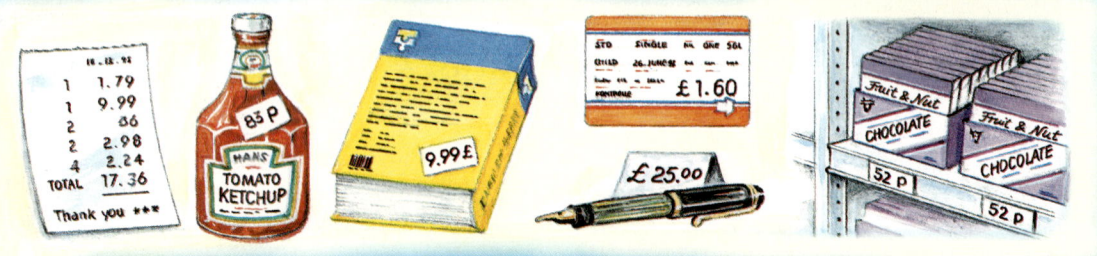

Shopping in Paulsgrove

UNIT 7

A

Our shop

by Madur Patel

Our shop - well, it's really my brother's shop - sells newspapers, magazines, cigarettes, sweets, drinks and chocolate. It's an English corner shop really, but we sell Asian food, too, and that's new in Paulsgrove.

Ramesh and I live with our parents. We've got a flat above the shop. Our parents are Indian but Ramesh and I are British. Portsmouth is our home. We love Britain but our parents aren't really happy here.

Ramesh opens the shop at eight in the morning and he only closes it at eight in the evening. People in Paulsgrove like that. "The other shops close at six and we can't buy Asian food in them," they say.

Things are fine really. But there is one problem. I like our corner shop. It's nice and small. But my brother wants a big shop one day.

A1 What's right?

1 The Patels sell
2 They sell
3 The Patels live
4 Ramesh and Madur are
5 Their parents are
6 Ramesh and Madur love Britain but
7 Ramesh opens the shop
8 He closes it
9 The other shops close
10 People can do their shopping
11 Ramesh wants

a) a big shop.
b) Asian food, too.
c) at eight in the evening.
d) at eight in the morning.
e) at six in the evening.
f) British.
g) in a flat above the shop.
h) Indian.
i) in the morning or in the evening.
j) newspapers, magazines, cigarettes, sweets, drinks and chocolate.
k) their parents aren't happy.

UNIT 7

Shopping in Paulsgrove

At the shop

John: Is that all, Alec?
Alec: Tea, coffee, matches, milk, dog food, bananas. Yes, that's all.
John: What about the sugar?
Alec: Oh, yes. A bag of sugar. Here it is.

John: How much is that, Ramesh?
Ramesh: That's £6.45.
John: Here you are.
Ramesh: Thanks. And here's your change, 55p.

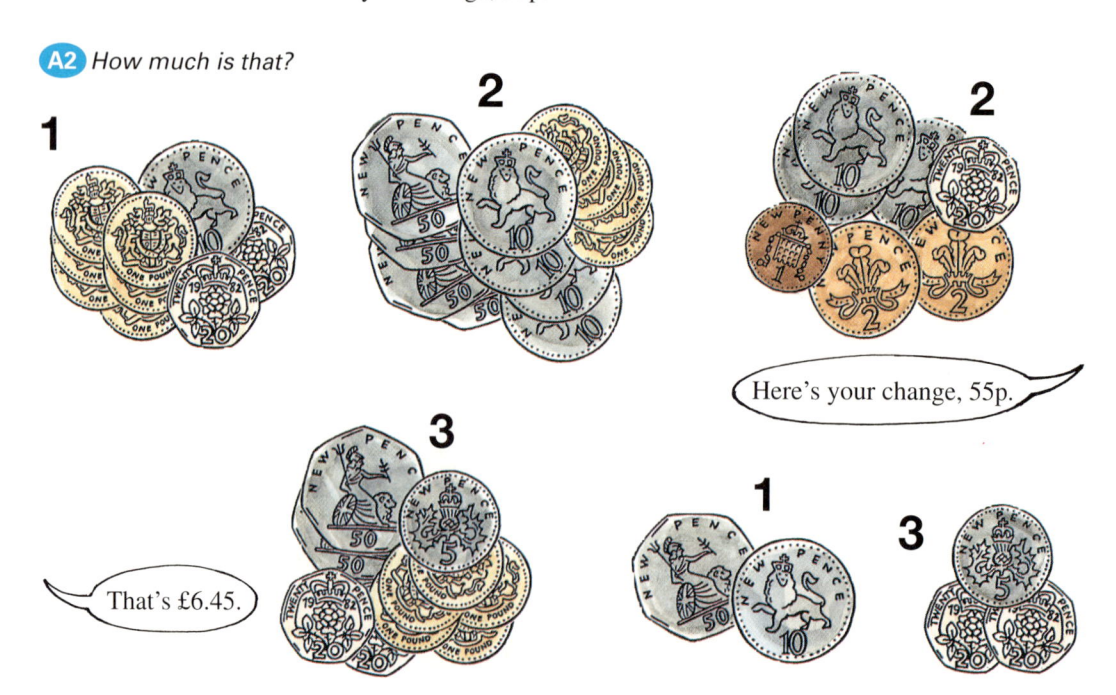

A2 How much is that?

Here's your change, 55p.

That's £6.45.

80 eighty

Shopping in Paulsgrove

UNIT 7

B

B1 *Talk about the people.*

do - go - help - like - play - visit

John and Grant are good friends. They ... their homework together. They ... to school together every morning. They've got a nice teacher. They ... football and squash. They ... Kim and Pat. They often ... Len in Portchester. They ... him and his dog and monkey. They ... him in the garden and sometimes ... his shopping.

B2 *What are they saying?*

I	buy	Len in the garden	on Fridays.
We	go	fish and chips	on ....
	help	football	every day.
	play	in my brother's shop	
	work	to my club	
		to the judo club	

	MON	TUES	WED	THURS	FRI	SAT	SUN
Len				*			
Mr Christian	*	*	*	*	*	*	*
Madur						*	
Grant and John							*
Robby Rob					*		
Kim and Pat		*					

B3 *Now you.*

I	often	watch TV	on	Saturdays.
	always	go to the sports centre		Sundays.
	sometimes	visit friends		
		play ...		
		help my mum		
		do the shopping		
		...		

UNIT 7

Shopping in Paulsgrove

B4 *Now you. Talk about your school.*

| On | Mondays
Tuesdays
... | I
we | come to school at
go home from school at
go to school from | ... o'clock.
half past ...
... to ... |

B5 *Now you. Talk about your family.*

| My | father
mother
brother
sister | works
goes to school
comes home | from ... to ...
at ... |

B6 *Talk to your partner.*

1 **bottle of milk – two boxes of matches – 41p**

A: Good morning. Can I help you?
B: Good morning. I'd like a bottle of milk, please.
A: Is that all?
B: No, I'd like two boxes of matches, please.
A: Here you are.
B: How much is that?
A: That's 41 pence, please.

2 **tin of dog food – newspaper – 65p**

A: Good morning. Can ...?
B: ... I'd like ..., please.
A: Is that ...?
B: No, ..., please.
A: Here ...
B: How much ...?
A: That's ...

3 **packet of tea - six bananas - £1.32**

A: ...
B: ...

B7 *Words: food or drink?*

banana - cake - chocolate - coffee - milk - sweets - tea - vegetables

B8 *Words: two together.*

| he | brother | dad | ... |
| she | ... | ... | mother |

B9 *Let's say it.*

[əʊ]

1 Is the r**o**bot ph**o**ning C**o**co?
2 Is C**o**co doing his h**o**mework? I d**o**n't kn**o**w.
3 Is the r**o**bot doing j**u**do? N**o**.
4 Let's g**o** to the r**o**bot sh**o**w!

[æ] or [e]?

1 Let's visit R**a**mesh in his fl**a**t.
2 What's the m**a**tter? T**e**ll me. - No, you **a**ren't my fri**e**nd.
3 Look at th**a**t. Your tyre is fl**a**t.
4 Who's th**a**t? T**e**ll me. - That's R**a**mesh Patel.

[v] or [w]?

1 **W**ell, that's a **v**ery good **v**ideo.
2 **W**hat a good **v**ideo!
3 **W**e're **v**isiting a **v**ery nice **w**oman.
4 **W**e play **v**olleyball every **w**eek.

82 eighty-two

Shopping in Paulsgrove UNIT 7

C

1 Was man beim Einkaufen sagt

Can I help you?	*Kann ich dir/euch/Ihnen helfen?*
I'd like a bottle of milk, please.	*Ich möchte bitte eine Flasche Milch.*
How much is that, please?	*Wieviel macht das, bitte?*
That's £1.50.	*Das macht ein Pfund fünfzig.*
Is that all, please?	*Ist das alles, bitte?*
Here you are.	*Bitteschön.* (beim Überreichen von Waren oder Geld)

2 Einfache Gegenwart (Present Simple)
   Sagen, was jemand immer, im Allgemeinen oder regelmäßig macht

I live in a flat. **She/It likes** bananas.
You always **buy** chocolate. **We live** with our parents.
Ramesh Patel sells newspapers and magazines. **They get** Asian food in Ramesh Patel's shop.

I You We They	live	in a house.	He She It	lives	in a house.

▶ *Grammar S. 123, 2*

D

D1 Picnic day for teddy bears

1 Read the text.

a) Boys and girls and their mothers and fathers like picnics.
b) But teddy bears love them. And every year the teddy bears have their picnic in the wood.
c) It's picnic day for teddy bears.
   They pay their money
   and eat bread and honey.
d) They drink their tea,
   very nice tea.
e) They dance and dance
   (Yes, bears can dance!).
f) In the evening they go home and they're happy little teddy bears.

2 Match the pictures to the sentences.

UNIT 7

Shopping in Paulsgrove

D2 At the shops

1. Listen to the cassette.
2. Write Coco's shopping list.
3. What's right?

   a) Coco goes into the | greengrocer's.
                         | newsagent's.
                         | supermarket.

   b) He wants ... at the ...
      He buys ... at ...
   c) The sweets are ...p.
      The apples and bananas are ...p.

D3 Your shop

Write about a shop in your town.
This list can help you.

The shop's name.
Where's the shop?
The shop sells ...
It opens at ...
It closes at ...
I often/sometimes go there.
I go there on ...
I buy ... there.

D4 Act the scene

A und B sind Kunden.
C ist Verkäufer(in) bzw. Ladenbesitzer(in).
A und B machen sich eine Einkaufsliste und kaufen bei C ein.
C legt die Preise fest.

C:	Begrüße A und B.
A&B:	Begrüßt C.
C:	Frage die Kunden nach ihren Wünschen.
A:	Nenne die ersten zwei Waren auf deiner Liste.
C:	Überreiche die Ware. Frage, ob das alles ist.
B:	Nenne die nächste Ware auf der Liste.
C:	Überreiche die Ware. Frage, ob das alles ist.
A&B:	Geht eure Liste Punkt für Punkt durch, während C die Waren überreicht und die Preise nennt. Dann sagt, dass das alles ist.
C:	Sage, wieviel das macht.
A:	Überreiche das Geld.
C:	Bedanke dich. Verabschiede dich.
A&B:	Verabschiedet euch.

Time for activities

1 The four seasons and the months

Look at the pictures and read the words.

1
Spring
March
April
May

2
Summer
June
July
August

3
Autumn
September
October
November

4
Winter
December
January
February

2 Words: make two lists.

1 Schreibe zehn Wörter auf, die dich an den Sommer, und zehn, die dich an den Winter erinnern.

Vielleicht denkst du bei diesen Wörtern an den Sommer:

drink swimming green T-shirt

Und vielleicht denkst du bei diesen Wörtern an den Winter:

white football television pullover

2 Jetzt lies deine Listen vor. Wissen deine Mitschüler, welche Liste sich auf den Sommer und welche Liste sich auf den Winter bezieht?

UNIT 8

The Paulsgrove Carnival

Labels in top illustration: jeans, dress, pullover, hat, blouse, T-shirt, skirt, coat

That's smart!

Labels in bottom illustration: shirt, jacket, cap, socks, trousers, shoes

1 *Talk about the people.*

1 She's got a hat on and ...
2 He's got a cap on and ...
3 She's ...

2 *What's your opinion?*

The girl's uniform	is	smart.
The boy's uniform	are	nice.
The trousers		awful.
The skirt		...
The socks		
The hat		

3 *What's your opinion?*

Was könnten das für Uniformen sein?
Was meint ihr?

4

She likes wearing her uniform.
He likes going to school, but he hates wearing his uniform.

The Paulsgrove Carnival

UNIT 8

Colours

black   brown   blue   green   yellow   violet   red   pink   white   grey

4 *Ask and answer.*

coat - jacket - hat - cap - shirt

1 A: What colour is the girl's (hat)?
   B: It's ...
2 A: What colour is the boy's (jacket)?
   B: It's ...
3 ...

5 *Ask and answer.*

socks - shoes - trousers - jeans

1 A: What colour are the (girl's) ...?
   B: They're ...
2 ...

6 *Now you. Play the game.*

A: I can see a (T-shirt).
B: Is it (red)?
A: Yes, it is.
   No, it isn't.
B: Has (Silvia) got it on?
A: Yes, (she) has.
   No, (she) hasn't.

A

Carnival in Paulsgrove

Part 1

Pat: Hello, Kim.
Kim: Oh, hello, Pat.
Pat: Where are you going?
Kim: I'm going to the club. To the Twirlettes group.
      We're in the big carnival parade next Saturday.
      Do you like the Twirlettes?
Pat: No, I don't. I think they're silly.
      Do you like that awful uniform?
Kim: Yes, I do. Anyway, it isn't awful. I think it's nice.
Pat: What about Rick? Does he like it?
Kim: Well, no, he doesn't. He only likes judo.

→ A1

eighty-seven 87

UNIT 8

The Paulsgrove Carnival

Part 2

Photographer:	Excuse me, please. Can you tell me the way to the Grove Club?
Pat:	Are you from the newspaper?
Photographer:	That's right.
Pat:	Why are you here?
Photographer:	I want to take a photo of the Twirlettes for the newspaper.
Pat:	They're silly. I hate watching them.
Photographer:	Well, that's your opinion. I love watching them. Their uniform is smart. Now, where's the Grove Club, please?
Pat:	It's easy. Go down this road to the traffic lights. Cross the road. Then turn left. That's Marsden Road.
Photographer:	Sorry. Marsdown?
Pat:	No, Marsden, M-A-R-S-D-E-N.
Photographer:	Oh, Marsden Road. Okay.
Pat:	The club is on the right.
Photographer:	Thank you.

→ A2

A1 What's right?

Kim	likes	judo.
Rick		the Twirlettes.
		the uniform.

A2 What's right?

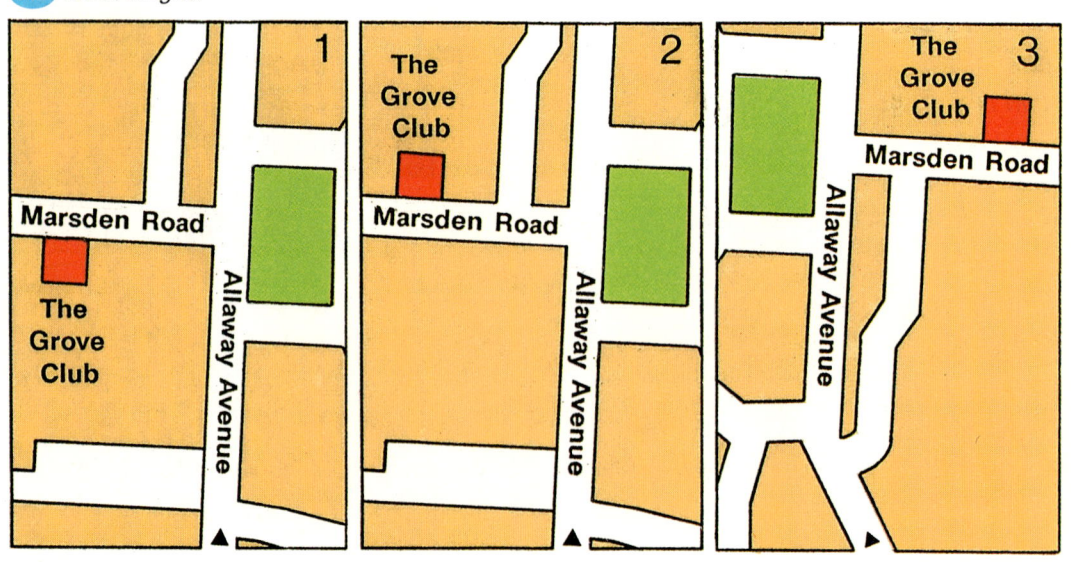

The Paulsgrove Carnival

UNIT 8

B

B1 *Ask and answer.*

1 A: Do you play (tennis)?
　B: Yes, I do.
　　 No, I don't.
2 A: Do you watch (football) on TV?
　B: Yes, I do.
　　 No, I don't.
3 …

volleyball   football   basketball   squash …

B2 *Ask and answer.*

1 I like Italian food.
　A: I like Italian food.
　　 Do you like it, too?
　B: Yes, I do./No, I don't.
2 I like sweets.
3 I like fish.
4 I like chocolate.
5 I like Turkish food.
6 …

B3 *Ask and answer.*

1 A: Does (Kim) like (chocolate)?
　B: Yes, (she) does.
　　 No, (she) doesn't.
2 A: Does (John) like (bananas)?
　B: …
3 …

	Kim	Pat	Mrs Fielding	John	Len	Grant
chocolate	*				*	*
bananas	*	*			*	*
honey			*	*		
fish and chips	*	*	*		*	
Indian food			*	*	*	

B4 *Now you. Talk about your family and friends.*

A: Does your | mother | like …?
　　　　　　　　| father | play …?
　　　　　　　　| sister | watch …?
　　　　　　　　| brother |
　　　　　　　　| friend |
　　　　　　　　| … |

B: Yes, he/she …
　 No, he/she …

basketball   football   tennis …

B5 *Now you.*

1 A: Do you like (dogs)?
　B: Yes, I do.
　　 No, I don't.
　A: What about your father/sister/…?
　　 Does he/she like (dogs)?
　B: Yes, he/she does.
　　 No, he/she doesn't.
2 …

dogs   computers   drinking coffee   eating chocolate   playing tennis   Christmas …

UNIT 8

The Paulsgrove Carnival

B6 *Ask and answer.*

A: Do they like (honey)?
B: Yes, they do.
   No, they don't.

B7 *Ask and answer.*

Look at the pictures.

"Turn right at the church."
"Go down this road."
"It's on the right."
"Cross the road."
"Turn left at the church."
"It's on the left."

Now ask and answer.

1 A: Can you tell me the way to the club, please?
   B: Go down ..., turn left at ... It's on the ...

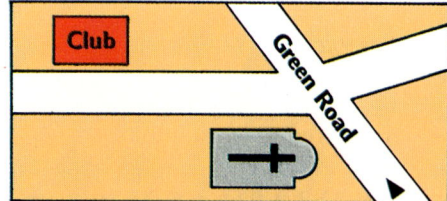

2 A: Can you tell me the way to the cinema, please?
   B: Cross ..., turn ... It's on the ...

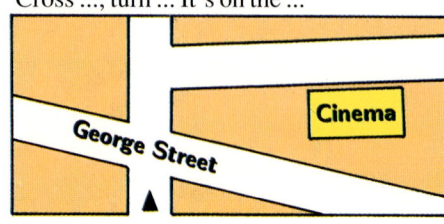

3 A: Can you tell me the way to the sports centre, please?
   B: Go down ..., turn ... at the traffic lights. It's on the ...

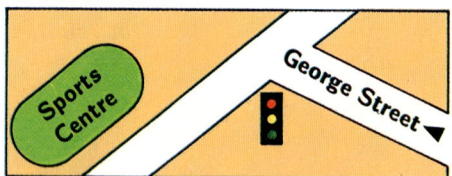

4 A: Can you tell me the way to the church, please?
   B: Turn ... at the cinema, ... Green Road, cross ..., turn ... It's on the ...

90 ninety

The Paulsgrove Carnival

UNIT 8

B8 *Now you. Talk about your town.*

Ask your partner the way from your school to the:

1 station
2 swimming pool
3 post office
4 ...

1 A: Can you tell me the way to the station?
   B: ...
2 ...

B9 *Listen to the ABC-Song and learn the letters.*

```
        ABC
    ABCDEFG
    HIJKLMNOP
    QRSTUV
    WXYZ.
```

a [eɪ]	j [dʒeɪ]	s [es]
b [biː]	k [keɪ]	t [tiː]
c [siː]	l [el]	u [juː]
d [diː]	m [em]	v [viː]
e [iː]	n [en]	w [ˈdʌbljuː]
f [ef]	o [əʊ]	x [eks]
g [dʒiː]	p [piː]	y [waɪ]
h [eɪtʃ]	q [kjuː]	z [zed]
i [aɪ]	r [ɑː]	

B10 *Say the letters.*

1 USA   4 EC
2 GB   5 BBC
3 UK   6 ABC

B11 *Spell the names.*

1 Otfried Bäßler
   A: Otfried Bäßler.
   B: Can you spell that, please?
   A: Yes. B - A-Umlaut - double-S - L - E - R.
   B: Bäßler. Thank you.

2 Your name
3 Your road
4 Your town

(nn = double-n
ß = double-s
ä = a-Umlaut or ae)

B12 *Words: what is Len saying?*

1 Mr is Christian is smart.
   He's got a blue hat on.
2 He's got ... on.
3 ...

B13 *Let's say it.*

[tʃ]

1 **Ch**air, wat**ch**, **ch**ips, **ch**ocolate, Fren**ch**, **ch**ur**ch**.
2 I'm sitting in my **ch**air and wat**ch**ing TV.
3 I'm sitting in my **ch**air and eating **ch**ips.

[dʒ]

1 **G**erman, **j**eans, **j**acket, **j**ar.
2 You can get good **j**eans and **j**ackets in Portsmouth.
3 **J**ohn isn't **G**erman.

B14 *Make two lists: [tʃ] or [dʒ]?*

chocolate - **Fr**ench - **j**acket - **G**erman - pic**tu**re - tea**ch**er - **ch**urch - **j**ar

[tʃ]	[dʒ]
change	**j**eans
...	...
...	

UNIT 8

C

The Paulsgrove Carnival

1 Fragen mit do/does (Questions with do/does)

Do you like white hats? *Magst du weiße Hüte?*
Do you like the Twirlettes? Yes, **I do**.
  No, **I don't**.
Does Rick like the uniform? Yes, **he does**.
  No, he doesn't.

| Do | I you we they | like carnivals? | Yes, | I you we they | do. | No, | I you we they | don't. |

| Does | he she it | like carnivals? | Yes, | he she it | does. | No, | he she it | doesn't. |

➤ *Grammar S. 121, 1a; S. 122, 1b/c; S. 130, 3c*

2 ing-Form als Nomen (ing-form as a noun)

I hate watch**ing** carnivals. Ich hasse es, Karnevalszüge anzugucken.
I love watch**ing** them. Ich liebe es, sie anzugucken.
I like swimm**ing**. Ich mag Schwimmen.

➤ *Grammar S. 122, 1b/c; S. 125, 1a*

3 Nach dem Weg fragen

Excuse me, please. Can you tell me the way to the cinema? *Entschuldigen Sie bitte. Können Sie mir sagen, wie ich zum Kino komme?*
Go down King Street. *Gehen Sie die Königstraße entlang. (1)*
Cross Station Road. *Überqueren Sie die Bahnhofstraße. (1)*
Turn right at the club. *Biegen Sie am Club rechts ab. (1)*
The cinema is **on the left**. *Das Kino ist auf der linken Seite. (1)*
Turn left at the club. *Biegen Sie am Club links ab. (2)*
The cinema is **on the right**. *Das Kino ist auf der rechten Seite. (2)*

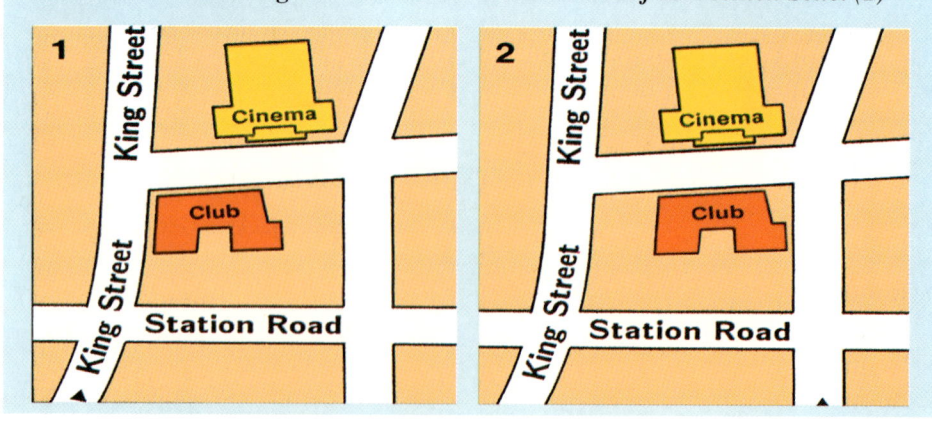

The Paulsgrove Carnival

UNIT 8

D

18th June

Dear Grandma,
Thank you for the wonderful flowers on my birthday. How are you? We're all fine here. I'm very busy, too. The Paulsgrove Summer Carnival is next Saturday. Do you like carnivals? I do. My Twirlettes group is in the big parade. It's always fun and everybody has a great time. There is a funfair, too, and a lot of stalls with games and food and drink. In the evening there is always a band and everybody dances. It's a wonderful carnival.
Well, that's all for now. It's late and I'm very tired.
Love,
Kim

D1 A letter to grandma

1 Read the letter.

2 Please answer.
a) What day is the carnival?
b) Where is it?
c) Does Kim like carnivals?
d) What can people do in the evening?

D2 A festival in your town

Now write a letter to a friend about a festival in your town. Look at Kim's letter for help.

D3 🎞 The big parade

1 Listen to the cassette.

2 In welcher Reihenfolge werden die sechs Straßen und Gebäude genannt?

a) Allaway Avenue
b) Castle School
c) The Green
d) The Grove Club
e) Marsden Road
f) Service Road

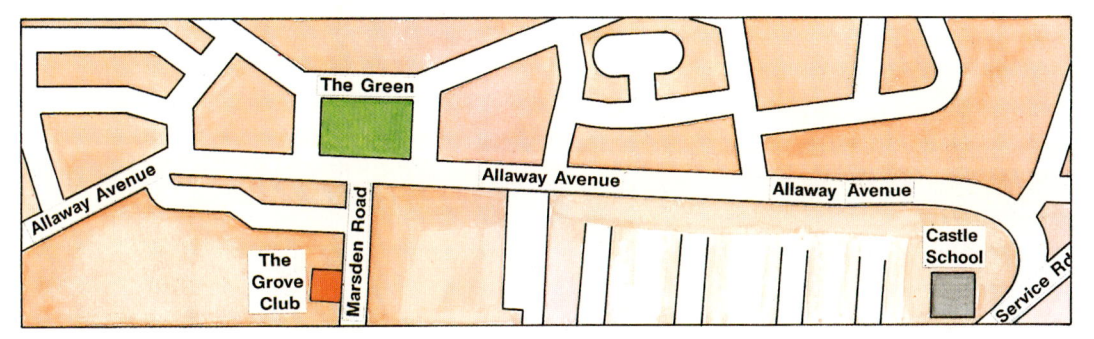

UNIT 8

The Paulsgrove Carnival

D4 ii Act the scene

1 Ask and answer.

A: Begrüße B.

B: Begrüße A.

A: Frage B, wie man zum Kino kommt.

B: Frage A, ob er/sie die Verkehrsampel sehen kann.

A: Sage, du kannst sie sehen.

B: Sage A, er/sie muss die Straße dort überqueren, dann nach links gehen. Das Kino ist auf der rechten Seite.

A: Bedanke dich und verabschiede dich von B.

B: Verabschiede dich.

2 Now you.

A: Frage B, wie man von der Schule zum/zur ... in deiner Stadt kommt.

B: Erkläre A den Weg.

A: Wiederhole, was B dir sagt.

B: Sage, das ist richtig.

B: Sage, das ist falsch, und wiederhole die Beschreibung.

A: Bedanke dich.

A: Bedanke dich.

Time for activities

1 Funny rhymes

Please read.

1 It's raining, it's pouring

It's raining. It's pouring.
The old man is snoring.
He went to bed
And bumped his head,
And couldn't get up in the morning.

it's pouring = *es regnet in Strömen*
to snore = *schnarchen*
went = *ging*
bumped = *stieß an*
couldn't = *konnte nicht*

Fuzzy Wuzzy

2

Fuzzy Wuzzy was a bear.
A bear was Fuzzy Wuzzy.
When Fuzzy Wuzzy lost his hair,
He wasn't fuzzy, was he?

fuzzy = *struppig*
was = war
lost = *verlor*
hair = *Haare*

3 Tick tock

Tick tock
Goes the clock,
Telling the time,
All by itself.
Round and round
The two hands go,
The big one quick,
The little one slow.

all by itself = *ganz allein*

Time for activities

2 The weather

1 Read the rhyme. 2 Kannst du den Reim auf Deutsch erklären?

> Red sky at night,
> shepherd's delight.
> Red sky in the morning,
> Shepherd's warning.

shepherd = *Schäfer*   delight = *Freude*   warning = *Warnung*

3 Tongue-Twisters

1 Red lorry, yellow lorry,
  red lorry, yellow lorry …

lorry = *Lastwagen*

2 Thirty-three feathers on a thrush's throat.

thrush = *Drossel*   throat = *Kehle*

4 Time for fun

Why is winter so long?

It comes in one year and goes out the other.

Who's that?

That's my tran-SISTER.

5 Game: "I spy"

A: I spy with my little eye something beginning with P.
B: Is is a pen?
A: No, it isn't.
C: Is it a pencil?
A: Yes, it is.
C: Okay. I spy with my little eye something beginning with…

I spy… = *Ich sehe was, das du nicht siehst, und das beginnt mit …*
something = *etwas*

I spy with my little eye something beginning with P.

Time for activities

6 Talk about the Patels and the Harmans?

7 What are the words?

1 Please complete the words.

a – e – i – o – u

a) y*ll*w
b) h*mst*r
c) t*nn*s
d) l*g
e) m*lk
f) br*th*r
g) b*sk*tb*ll
h) gr**n
i) h**d
j) s*st*r
k) b**r
l) w*t*r

2 What words go together?

a) yellow   –   green
b) hamster –   …
c) …

8 A secret message

1 First look at this code.

1	2	3	4	5	6	7	8	9	10
Z	Y	X	W	V	U	T	S	R	Q

11	12	13	14	15	16	17	18	19	20
P	O	N	M	L	K	J	I	H	G

21	22	23	24	25	26
F	E	D	C	B	A

2 Can you read the message?

4 9 18 7 22 STOP
2 12 6 9 STOP 13 26 14
22 STOP 26 13 23 STOP
20 18 5 22 STOP 18 7
STOP 7 12 STOP 7 19 22
STOP 7 22 26 24 19 22
9 STOP

Do it! The first is the winner!

3 Now write your partner an English message in code. Can he/she read it?

Magazine 2

Do you watch too much TV?

	No	Yes
● You know the words of all the ads.	0	15
● You never sing the songs in the ads.	20	0
● You know the real names of film stars.	0	5
● Your favourite programme is on TV but you play sport with your friends.	30	0
● You never switch off the TV before 9 o'clock in the evening and read a book.	0	10
● You watch all the programmes with mum and dad.	0	20

How many points have you got?
0–20 You're okay. You don't watch too much TV.
21–40 You're normal.
41–60 Whoah! This is already a problem.
61–80 Haven't you got friends?
81–100 Sorry, you watch too much TV.

Magazine 2

Come to the circus!

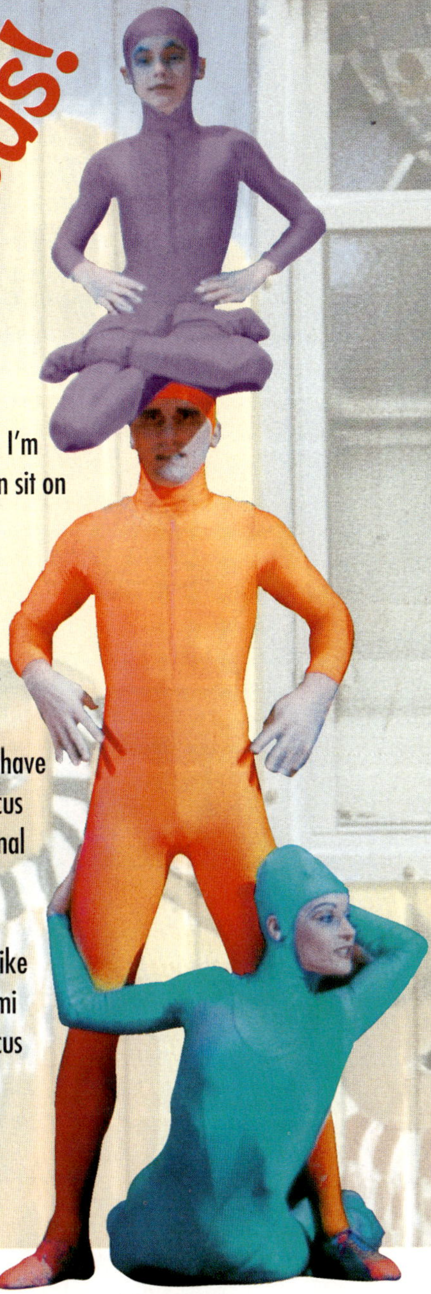

This is Anton. He's a circus boy.

"I'm ten years old and I'm the youngest person in the circus. I'm an acrobat. I'm in a part of the show with my mother and father. I'm only thirty kilos so I can sit on my father's head in the show.

My day starts at 8 o'clock. I have breakfast at 8 o'clock. I often have bacon and eggs. I have a normal lunch and a small dinner before the show in the evening. I have school from 10 o'clock in the morning to 4 o'clock in the afternoon. Then I do training for an hour with my mother and father. Dinner is at 6 o'clock and then it's time for the evening show.

I can't go to a normal school. I have a private teacher. We are a circus family. We don't live in a normal house. Our home is a family trailer. We sometimes have famous people in the show, like Arnold Schwarzenegger, Demi Moore and Bruce Willis. Circus life is a lot of fun."

Is circus life for you? What are you good at?

swimming  · swimming under water  · judo  · climbing  · diving  · boxing  · dancing  · acrobatics

Are you good at dancing?

I'm	good at not bad at all right at …	that

Do you like	living in a trailer? going to school? …
Yes, I do. No, I don't.	I've got no idea. I don't know.

ninety-nine 99

MAGAZINE 2

Mum: Joey, go and play with your drum in the street. Your father can't read his newspaper.
Joey: Huh! I'm only seven and I can read it.

Mum: Barbara, what are you doing out there in the rain?
Barbara: I'm getting wet!

Girl: Can you jump higher than that wall?
Boy: Yes, sure. That wall can't jump.

Jimmy: Mum! The kids at school call me Bighead.
Mum: Don't listen to them. Bring me five kilos of potatoes in your cap from the shop.

Man: How much to the station?
Taxi driver: Fifty pence, sir.
Man: And how much for my bag?
Taxi driver: It's free.
Man: Right. Then take my bag to the station. I'll walk.

MAGAZINE 2

Your letters

A new idea
Why are books so expensive? My grandmother gave me a book for my birthday. It's called 'The Babysitters Club, Kristy and the snobs'. It was a really good story. Then in the shop I saw a lot of other books about the Babysitters Club. I wanted more Babysitters books but they were expensive. I talked to my friends and we all had the same problem so we started a Book Club. We take our old books to the Book Club and get tickets for the price – one ticket for one pound. We 'buy' a new book with our tickets and then we can take it home. So we only buy one book but we can read a lot of books!
David

Boring
Why are there so many stories about the Queen and the Royal Family in the newspapers and on TV? They're really boring. Why can't they write about normal people?
Pat

- That's a great idea, David. Maybe other kids can start Book Clubs, too.

- A lot of people like stories about the Royals, Pat. I don't like reading about them. Maybe you can do what I do – listen to music or play sport.

Here I am on holiday in Portsmouth. I'm having a great time. I'm staying at my cousin's house. Her name is Susan. Her school holidays started last week, so we can do things together. Yesterday we visited the centre of Portsmouth. We looked at the Victory. Then we went to the swimming pool because the sea isn't very nice here. There is a circus in town this week. Maybe we will go there this evening. I've got two more weeks here. So, that's my idea of a good holiday. What is your idea of a good holiday?
Harriet

- Thanks for your holiday postcard, Harriet. My idea of a good holiday? That's easy – I like going to discos and sleeping in the sun by the sea! Anything else? Oh, I love ice cream. You, too?

What about you?
– Do you like David's idea?
– What do you think of the Royals?
– What is your idea of a good holiday?

UNIT 9

People far and near

1 Inverness

Loch Dochort 2

What season is it?
spring – summer – autumn – winter
1 Number one is ...
2 ...

Forest Park, Glenmore 4

Scotland
– the four seasons

3 Edinburgh, Princes Street

People far and near

UNIT 9

A

The Scottish boy

Part 1

Girl: Alec. We're from the school magazine. Can we ask you some questions?
Alec: Yes, of course.
Boy: Well, first, where do you live?
Alec: In King Street.
Boy: Where do you come from originally, Alec?
Alec: From Glasgow in Scotland.
Girl: Where do your mum and dad work?
Alec: Well, my dad works on the ferries to France. And my mother is a housewife. But she's looking for a job.
Boy: What do you speak at home? English?
Alec: Yes, of course.
Girl: Not Gaelic?
Alec: Oh, no! My mother knows a few words. You've got funny ideas about the Scots.

→ A1

Part 2

Girl: Do you play the bagpipes?
Alec: The bagpipes? No, I don't.
Boy: What about kilts? Have you got a kilt?
Alec: No. But my dad has got a kilt. It's red, green and blue.
Boy: When does he wear it?
Alec: Well, he doesn't wear it very often.

Part 3

Girl: What about Portsmouth? Do you and your parents like it?
Alec: Well, my mum doesn't like the shops here. And my dad doesn't like the pubs. But they like the people, yes.
Boy: And what about you? Do you like school?
Alec: I don't like some teachers. But it's okay.
Boy: What subject do you like best?
Alec: Oh, that's easy. Maths is my favourite subject.
Girl: And one last question, Alec. Do you miss Scotland?
Alec: Yes, sometimes.

→ A2

one hundred and three 103

UNIT 9

People far and near

A1 What's right?

1 Alec Ross
2 The boy and girl
3 They work for
4 Alec lives in
5 His dad works on
6 His mother

a) are from the school magazine.
b) is a housewife.
c) comes from Glasgow.
d) the school magazine.
e) King Street.
f) the ferries to France.

A2 Here is the magazine story about Alec. What's missing?

NEW BOY FROM SCOTLAND

Alec Ross ... the new Scottish boy in our school. He ... in King Street. He ... from Glasgow originally. Alec's father ... on the ferries, and his mother ... a housewife. They ... English at home, but his mother ... a few words of Gaelic.
Alec is Scottish but he doesn't ... the bagpipes and he ... got a kilt. His dad ... got a kilt, but he doesn't ... it very often. His mum and dad ... the people in Portsmouth. Alec ... school but he ... all his teachers. His favourite subject is Maths.

B

B1 What are they saying?

1 *Alec:*   I like Maths best.
2 *Rita:*   I like ...
3 *Grant:* ...
4 *Kim:*   ...
5 *John:*   ...
6 *Pat:*   ...

Favourite subjects:

Alec	-	Maths
Rita	-	Drama
Grant	-	Music
Kim	-	Physical Education (P.E.)
John	-	English
Pat	-	Food and Fitness

B2 Now you.

A: Where do you go | in the afternoon?
                   | on Saturdays?
                   | on Sundays?

B: I go to the (sports centre). What about you?
A: ...

UNIT 9

People far and near

B3 *Ask and answer.*

1. John: When do you play (tennis), Kim?
   Kim: On (Tuesday).
2. Pat: When do you play (football), Grant?
   Grant: ...
3. Mark: ...
   ...
4. Kim: ...
   ...
5. Alec: ...
   ...
6. Grant: ...
   ...
7. ...

	MON	TUES	WED	THURS	FRI	SAT	SUN
Kim		Tennis			Basketball		
John	Squash		Football				
Pat				Volleyball	Basketball		
Mark		Tennis					Football
Grant		Tennis	Football				Football
Alec	Squash			Volleyball			

B4 *Now you.*

A: What subject do you like best?
   When   play (football)?
   Where   go on Saturday?

B: I like ...
   play ...
   go ...

B5 *Ask and answer.*

1. What subject does Alec like best? — Maths.
2. Where ... he live? — In King Street.
3. What ... he speak at home? — English.
4. Where ... his father work? — On the ferries.
5. When ... his father wear his kilt? — Not very often.
6. What ... Alec miss sometimes? — Scotland.

Riddle

What goes 99 tap ~ 1 plonk ...?

A centipede with a wooden leg.

UNIT 9

People far and near

B6 *Ask and answer.*

Alec's Thursday

1 A: When does Alec (go to school)? → 8.45 - go to school
   B: At (a quarter to nine).   12.00 - go home for lunch
2 A: Where does he (go at 3.25)?   12.55 - go to school again
   B: (He goes home.)   →   3.25 - go home
3 A: What does he (do at 5.30)?   4.00 - do homework
   B: ...   5.00 - go to the Mountbatten
4 ...   Centre
                                          → 5.30 - play volleyball
                                             7.30 - go home
                                             8.00 - watch TV/read
                                             9.00 - go to bed

B7 *Now you. Ask and answer.*

A: When does your | mother | go to school?   B: He (comes home) (at half past five).
                  | father | go to work?   She ...
                  | sister | come home?
                  | brother | go to bed?
                            | watch TV?
                            | play ...?

B8 *Talk about the people and pets.*

1 **The Twirlettes don't wear red uniforms.**   a) Their house is in Paulsgrove.
2 John and Grant don't visit Len on Sundays.   b) They're Len's pets.
3 Mark and Madur don't go to the judo club.   c) **Their uniform is blue.**
4 Mr and Mrs Ross don't live in Portchester.   d) They like swimming.
5 Mr Christian and Skipper don't go to   e) They go on Saturdays.
   school.

B9 *Talk about the people and pets.*

1 **Madur's father doesn't read**   a) He only speaks English.
   English newspapers.   b) She only likes water.
2 Alec Ross doesn't speak Gaelic.   c) It's always on Thursdays.
3 Len Bignall doesn't go to his club on   d) **He gets an Indian newspaper**
   Saturdays.   **every week.**
4 Madur's brother doesn't sell bananas.   e) He isn't a greengrocer.
5 Skipper doesn't drink tea.

People far and near

UNIT 9

B10 What's missing?

don't – doesn't

1 Pat ... like monkeys.

2 Kim ... like seagulls.

3 Mr and Mrs Smith ... like hamsters.

4 Seagulls ... like bears.

5 Skipper and Mr Christian ... like birds.

6 Alec ... like elephants.

B11 Make a survey.

1 Ask your partners:

   A: Do you like (volleyball)?
   B: Yes, I do.
   C: No, I don't.
   D: ...

volleyball	chocolate	hamsters
tennis	sugar	monkeys
football	honey	elephants
judo	sweets	dogs

2 Write the answers in a survey.

3 Now speak about your group:

(Five) people like ...
(Two) people don't like ...
One girl likes ...
Only one boy doesn't like ...

B12 Words: where is it?

in – on – under

1 It's ... the cupboard.
2 ...

B13 Let's say it.

[θ]
1 Can I have **th**ree pounds twenty, please. Oh, **th**ank you.
2 Grant **Sm**i**th** has got **Math**s at half past **th**ree on his bir**th**day.

[ð]
1 **Th**is tea is wi**th** sugar. Let's drink it toge**th**er.
2 Whose bro**th**er is **th**at? **Th**at's my fa**th**er's bro**th**er.

B14 Make two lists: [θ] or [ð]

thanks – Maths – with – this – birthday –
together – there – Thursday – that

[θ]	[ð]
three	fa**th**er
...	...

B15 Let's say it.

[s]
1 Let'**s** go and **s**ee the ferry.
2 My dad work**s** on the ferry.

[z]
1 She'**s** wearing blue shoe**s** and white trouser**s**.
2 Nice colour**s**!

[s]/[z]
1 Cro**ss** the road now, please.
2 Please, cro**ss** the road now.

B14 Make two lists: [s] or [z]

see – trousers – works – shoes – cross –
Scotland – please

[s]	[z]
bagpipers	colours
...	...

one hundred and seven 107

UNIT 9   People far and near

C

1 Fragen mit Fragewörtern und do/does (Questions with question words and do/does)

Where	do	you	live?	Wo wohnst du?
What	do	they	speak at home?	Was sprechen sie zu Hause?
When	does	your father	wear his kilt?	Wann trägt dein Vater seinen Kilt?

➤ Grammar S. 131, 3d

2 Verneinung mit don't/doesn't (Negation with don't/doesn't)

I	don't	like	some teachers.	He	doesn't	like	the pubs.
You			the Twirlettes.	She			the shops.
We			carnivals.	It			bears.
They			robots.				

➤ Grammar S. 122, 1c; S. 129, 2c

3 Das ist im Englischen anders:

I **don't** speak French.   Ich spreche **nicht** französisch.

➤ Grammar S. 122, 1c; S. 129, 2c

4 Steigerung (Comparison: Superlative)

small – small**er** – small**est**   klein – kleiner – am kleinsten
Peter is the **smallest** boy in the class.   Peter ist der **kleinste** Junge in der Klasse.
Sarah is the **biggest** girl in the class.   Sarah ist das **größte** Mädchen in der Klasse.

➤ Grammar S. 126, 3b

D

D1 Alec's timetable

Castle School

	Monday	Tuesday	Wednesday	Thursday	Friday
8.55	ASSEMBLY				
9.40	Maths	French / German	Maths	Maths	English
10.30	BREAK				
10.50	English	Reading	English	English	P.E. / Music
12.00	LUNCH				
1.05	French / German	Art	Science	Project	Writing
2.15	BREAK				
2.35	R.E. / Music	Food and Fitness	Games	Project	Drama / Computer Studies
3.25					

P. E. = Physical Education, R. E. = Religious Education

People far and near

UNIT 9

1 *Ask and answer.*

a) What time is Assembly?
b) What time is the morning break?
c) What time is the afternoon break?
d) What time is (Maths) on (Monday)?
e) What time ...

2 *Now you. What's different in your school?*

A: We've got ...
B: We haven't got ...
A: ...

3 *Write your timetable in English. Ask your teacher for the words.*

D2 An interview

1 *Mache ein Interview mit deinem Partner.*

– Zuerst stellst du Fragen an deinen Partner, dann macht er ein Interview mit dir.
– Redet über euch selbst oder spielt bekannte Popstars oder Sportler und denkt euch die Antworten aus.
– Was könnt ihr fragen?
  Unten findet ihr viele mögliche Fragen. Schaut sie euch an und sucht die Fragen aus, die ihr stellen möchtet.
– Es gibt keine feste Reihenfolge für eure Fragen. Achtet auf die Antworten eures Interviewpartners und stellt die nächste passende Frage.
– Notiert euch die Antworten.

Questions

Do you like	pop music? folk music? ...? English? Maths? ... ? dogs? ... ? hamburgers? tea? ... ?
Do you play	football? basketball? ...?

Do you	watch TV? ...?
When do you	get up? go to school? ...?
What do you do	in the afternoon? on Saturdays? ...?
Where do you	live? go to school? do your homework? ...?

What	music films sports books ...	do you	like? read? watch? buy? play? ...?

Have you got ...?   Can you ...?   ...?

2 *Berichte der Klasse anschließend über dein Interview.*

D3 Who's who?

1 *Bringe ein Kinderfoto von dir mit.*

2 *Schreibe über dich selbst, als ob du eine andere Person wärst:*

He/She likes ...
He/She plays ...
He/She lives ...
He/She ... on Saturdays.
...

3 *Mischt die Fotos und Texte.*

Who's who?

Time for a story

The clever crow

It was a lovely morning in spring. Fleet, the fox, was hungry. He wanted food.

He saw a nest up in a tree. There was a mother bird in it with her three baby birds.

"Hey, you up there," Fleet shouted. "Throw down one of your babies."

"No," the mother bird answered. "Go away, fox, go away."

"Right," Fleet shouted again. "I'm coming up for all four of you."

The mother bird was very afraid. But there was also a clever crow in the tree. The crow was the cleverest bird in the wood. She shouted, "It's all right, mother bird. The fox can't come up. He can't climb or fly."

The fox was angry and ran away.

Then one day he saw the crow. He was hungry ! He lay down on the ground and closed his eyes. "Is the fox dead?" the crow thought. But she was very clever. "Dead foxes have their eyes open," she shouted. Fleet opened his eyes. "You aren't dead," the crow said. "You're a fool!" She laughed and flew away. Now Fleet was very angry.

Later he saw the crow again. Now he had a plan. He lay down on the ground again. The crow saw him.

"Dead foxes have their eyes open," she shouted. But Fleet was clever. His eyes were closed. The crow came near, but Fleet's eyes were still closed.

So the crow jumped on to Fleet and shouted, "The fox is dead, the fox is dead!" Fleet caught her and ran into the wood.

"A crow is good food," he thought.

"Now," Fleet said to the crow, "this is the end. You're my dinner."

"That's all right," the crow said.

"Aren't you afraid?" Fleet asked. "No," said the crow. "You can eat me. I'm not afraid of that. But I am afraid of high rocks."

"That's a good idea," thought Fleet. He ran through the woods and came to the high rocks.

"Are you afraid now?" he asked.

"Oh yes," said the crow. "Please, please, eat me!"

"No," said Fleet. And he opened his mouth and threw the crow down from the rock. The crow fell, but then she flew away and laughed and laughed and laughed. Fleet was very angry. And very hungry.

Time for a story

Geschichten lesen

Du kennst bereits die Gegenwartsform (Present Simple) von vielen Zeitwörtern im Englischen und kannst über Ereignisse in der Gegenwart sprechen.
zum Beispiel:

They **go** to school every day.   *Sie **gehen** jeden Tag zur Schule.*
John **likes** computers.   *John **mag** Computer.*

Wenn du nun Geschichten lesen möchtest, musst du eine weitere Form des Zeitworts verstehen können: die Vergangenheitsform.

zum Beispiel:
She **came** home late.   *Sie **kam** spät nach Hause.*
John **opened** the door.   *John **öffnete** die Tür.*

Lies nun die Geschichte "The clever crow" und erzähle sie deinem Partner nachher auf Deutsch. Schreibe dann alle Vergangenheitsformen der Zeitwörter in dein Heft. Dabei kannst du feststellen, dass es im Englischen zwei Möglichkeiten gibt, die Vergangenheitsform der Zeitwörter zu bilden. Trage alle Beispiele in eine Liste ein und schreibe zum Vergleich immer die entsprechenden Formen des Present Simple dazu.

Regelmäßige Bildung der Vergangenheit durch das Anhängen von *-ed*		Unregelmäßige Bildung der Vergangenheit (neues Wort)	
Vergangenheit	Gegenwart	Vergangenheit	Gegenwart
wanted (want + ed)	want	was	is

▶ *Grammar S. 124, 5b*

Play

GHOST HUNTERS

Ghost hunters

Listen to the cassette. You can act this play in class, too.

The Class Play

GHOST HUNTERS

Grant Smith as *Lord Willis*
Kim Fielding as *Lady Willis*
Alec Ross as *Simon Carstairs*
Pat Miller as *Penny Sands*
Mark Harman as *the Ghost of Willis Hall!*

Scene one

WILLIS HALL TOURIST HOTEL

Carstairs: You've got a nice hotel here, Lord Willis. Very, very nice.
Lord Willis: Thank you, Mr Carstairs.

Carstairs: So, this is the room, eh?
Lord Willis: Yes, Mr Carstairs. This is the room. Our ghost room.
Carstairs: And when can we see the ghost?
Lady Willis: At twelve o'clock. It always comes at midnight.
Penny Sands: Is it dangerous, Lord Willis?

112 one hundred and twelve

PLAY

Lord Willis: I don't know, Miss Sands. Maybe it is, maybe it isn't. I never come to this room at midnight.
Carstairs: It's all right, Penny. I can do judo!
Penny Sands: Judo? Simon, you can't do judo with ghosts!
Lord Willis: Now, you must stay in the room and wait till midnight. Take some photos of the ghost when it comes. I've got to have some photos for my hotel brochure.
Penny Sands: Yes, a hotel with a ghost. Tourists really like ghosts.
Lady Willis: Yes. We haven't got many tourists but we need them. We need a lot of tourists. We need the money.
Penny Sands: I see.
Lord Willis: Now, have you got everything?
Penny Sands: Yes, Lord Willis. Yes, thank you.
Lord Willis: The telephone is here. You can phone me for help.
Penny Sands: Yes, of course.
Lady Willis: But please, you must take a photo of our ghost. Please!
Carstairs: Yes, yes. Of course, Lady Willis.
Lord Willis: Good night, Miss Sands.
Penny Sands: Good night.
Lord Willis: Good night, Mr Carstairs.
Carstairs: Good night, sir. Good night, madam.

Scene two

Eine Uhr tickt laut.
Carstairs: Well, here we are in the ghost room.
Penny Sands: Yes. What's the time?
Carstairs: Twenty to twelve.
Penny Sands: Is the telephone okay?
Carstairs hebt den Telefonhörer ab.
Carstairs: Yes, the phone is okay.
Penny Sands: Have you got the camera?
Carstairs: Yes, here it is.
Penny Sands: Look.
Carstairs: What's that?
Penny Sands: I've got my cassette-recorder here.
Carstairs: A cassette-recorder?! Pah. We haven't got time for music. Lord Willis wants some photos of the ghost.
Penny Sands: Mmm, I know, but ...
Carstairs: Ah well, let's sit down there and wait.
Penny Sands: No, let's sit here where the ghost can't see us.
Carstairs: Good idea.

Scene three

Carstairs pfeift vor sich hin.
Penny Sands: Simon.
Carstairs: What?
Carstairs pfeift weiter.
Penny Sands: Simon, please stop.
Carstairs: Oh. Sorry.
Carstairs: What's the time now?
Penny Sands: Oh, it's twelve o'clock. It's midnight. Brrr!
Eine Uhr schlägt zwölfmal.
Carstairs: He's late.
Penny Sands: No, wait! What's that?
Carstairs: Sssh! Shut up!
Penny Sands: There he is!

PLAY
Scene four

Ghost: Ooooh! Woo-hoooo! I am the ghost of Willis Hall. I walk at night when all men, women and children are sleeping. I am the Willis ghost. Oooh-hooo! Woo-hoo! There. That's my work for this evening. And now I can sleep, too.

Carstairs photographiert das Gespenst.

Carstairs: I've got it!
Ghost: What's that? What's happening? Who's there?

Carstairs macht eine zweite Aufnahme.

Carstairs: There. That's two photos. Thank you, Mr Ghost.
Ghost: Who are you?
Carstairs: Simon Carstairs.
Penny Sands: And I'm Penny Sands. And what's your name, Mr Ghost?
Ghost: I am Lord Cecil Willis. I am the ghost of Willis Hall. I am three hundred and twenty-five years old.
Penny Sands: Three hundred ...?
Ghost: ... and twenty-five. What have you got there?
Carstairs: This? It's a camera, Lord Cecil.
Ghost: Ooh. A "camera", eh? And what can you do with it?
Carstairs: You can take photos with it.
Ghost: Photos? Of me?
Carstairs: Yes. I've got two photos of you.
Ghost: Hah, hah! Hah! Really! Have you now? What fun!
Carstairs: Er ... yes. Lord Willis - er the new Lord Willis - has got to have some photos of you. He needs them for his hotel brochure.

PLAY

Ghost:	Pah, hotels!
Penny Sands:	Yes, tourists like ghosts. And Lord Willis wants the photo because he needs tourists.
Ghost:	Pah! Tourists! Do you like tourists?
Penny Sands:	Well, no, I don't. But Lord Willis needs the money.
Ghost:	Well, I'm sorry. You can't take photos of me.
Carstairs:	But I've got two photos of you here.
Ghost:	No, you haven't. I'm sorry. I'm a ghost. You can't take photos of ghosts.
Carstairs:	No?
Ghost:	No, no, my boy. Look at your photos.
Carstairs:	Oh, Penny. Look. He isn't on this photo.
Penny Sands:	And he isn't on this photo.
Carstairs:	Oh, no!
Ghost:	No, I'm sorry. You see? Your camera doesn't help because you can't take photos of ghosts. Ah, well. Time for bed. Good night, Mr Carstairs.
Carstairs:	Er ...
Ghost:	Good night, Miss Sands. And say hello to Lord Willis when you see him.
Penny Sands:	Yes. Good night, Lord Cecil. 'Night!

Scene five

Carstairs:	Oh dear, Penny. What can we do now? We haven't got the photos. We're terrible ghost hunters.
Penny Sands:	Oh, no, we aren't!
Carstairs:	Huh?
Penny Sands:	We're very good ghost hunters. Listen to this ...

> And what's your name, Mr Ghost?
> I am Lord Cecil Willis.
> I am the ghost of Willis Hall.
> I am three hundred and twenty-five years old.

Carstairs:	Hey, Penny! The cassette-recorder! What a great idea!

Penny hebt den Telefonhörer ab und wählt.

Lord Willis:	Hello.
Penny Sands:	Hello, Lord Willis. This is Penny Sands here. We've got your ghost.

Zweites Suchbild zu 3 auf Seite 34: What's the difference?

Hier und auf Seite 34 findet ihr zwei sehr ähnliche Bilder. Sie enthalten jedoch acht kleine Unterschiede, die ihr in Partnerarbeit herausfinden könnt. Einer von euch sieht das Bild auf dieser Seite an, der andere schlägt die Seite 34 auf. Fragt eueren Partner nach seinem Bild!

Have you got …?	Is … in/on …?
Has … got …?	I've got … in my picture. What about you?

wordfields

1 People

What a nice friend!

1. baby
2. child
3. girl
4. boy
5. pupil
6. woman
7. lady
8. man
9. partner
10. friend
11. neighbour
12. tourist
13. clown
14. housewife
15. newsagent
16. greengrocer
17. fisherman
18. sailor
19. postman
20. teacher
21. professor

Wow! That's a great ghost!

2 Feelings

How are you?
I'm fine.

1. fine
2. glad
3. happy
4. angry

What's the matter?
It's awful.

1. bad
2. boring
3. silly
4. awful

That's good!

1. nice
2. great
3. wonderful
4. fantastic
5. funny
6. clever

3 The body

Oh, my head hurts.

1. head
2. eye
3. mouth
4. arm
5. hand
6. finger
7. leg
8. foot

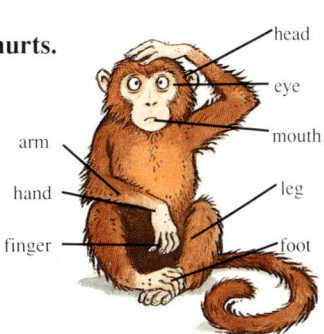

4 Food and drink

I'm hungry!
Well, you can eat bread...

1. bread
2. honey
3. biscuits
4. cakes
5. sugar
6. hamburgers
7. beef
8. fish
9. chips
10. vegetables
11. pies
12. apples
13. bananas
14. sweets
15. chocolate
16. nuts

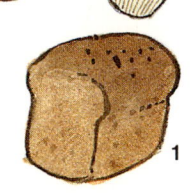

... and you can drink milk...

1. milk
2. water
3. tea
4. coffee

... for breakfast.

1. breakfast
2. lunch
3. teatime
4. dinner

one hundred and seventeen 117

Wordfields

5 Clothes

I'm wearing a shirt and red trousers.

1. cap
2. hat
3. blouse
4. skirt
5. dress
6. coat
7. shirt
8. pullover
9. jacket
10. trousers
11. jeans
12. socks
13. shoes

You're smart!

6 The family

This is my cousin.

1. grandmother
2. grandfather
3. mother (mum)
4. father (dad)
5. daughter
6. son
7. sister
8. brother
9. aunt
10. uncle
11. cousin

7 Pets and animals

John doesn't like crows.

1. bird
2. crow
3. hamster
4. dog
5. monkey
6. fox
7. bear
8. elephant

8 In the classroom

There's a rubber.

1. biro
2. pen
3. pencil
4. rubber
5. book
6. chair
7. desk
8. blackboard
9. window
10. door

9 Sports

My favourite sport is volleyball.

1. basketball
2. volleyball
3. football
4. tennis
5. squash
6. judo
7. swimming

10 It's fun!

I like comics.

1. hobby
2. song
3. quiz
4. poster
5. magazine
6. comic
7. camera
8. computer
9. cassette-recorder
10. stereo
11. television
12. video

I'm going to the sports centre.

1. picnic
2. party
3. park
4. game
5. swimming pool
6. sports centre
7. club
8. funfair
9. film
10. cinema
11. festival

118 one hundred and eighteen

Wordfields

11 What are they doing?

She's crossing the road.
They're playing football.

1. sitting
2. standing
3. lying down
4. walking
5. running
6. flying
7. falling
8. eating
9. drinking
10. talking
11. singing
12. reading
13. watching TV
14. babysitting
15. phoning
16. washing the car
17. playing basketball
18. crossing the road
19. shopping
20. selling vegetables

12 Colours

The shoes are green.

1. black
2. brown
3. blue
4. green
5. yellow
6. violet
7. red
8. pink
9. white
10. grey

13 The time of day

1. morning
2. afternoon
3. evening
4. day
5. night

14 The days of the week

Today is Wednesday.

1. Monday
2. Tuesday
3. Wednesday
4. Thursday
5. Friday
6. Saturday
7. Sunday

15 The months and the seasons

It's January.

1. January
2. February
3. March
4. April
5. May
6. June
7. July
8. August
9. September
10. October
11. November
12. December

1. spring
2. summer
3. autumn
4. winter

one hundred and nineteen 119

Grammar

Liebe Schülerin, lieber Schüler!

Auf den folgenden Seiten findest du noch einmal alles gesammelt, was du im ersten Band von ENGLISH LIVE an Grammatik durchnimmst. So kannst du unabhängig von der Unit, die gerade dran ist, alles nachschlagen und eventuell noch einmal lernen. Manches wird dir vielleicht auch klarer, wenn du es in der Übersicht siehst.

Auf dieser Seite findest du alphabetisch geordnet die wichtigsten grammatischen Bezeichnungen in Englisch, Deutsch und Latein. Englische und lateinische Bezeichnungen sind sich manchmal recht ähnlich. Damit du sie nicht verwechselst, sind die lateinischen Ausdrücke *schräg* gedruckt.

Übrigens: Der lustige Coco kann einfach seinen Mund nicht halten und redet immer dazwischen.
Aber sieh dir seine Sprüche ruhig genauer an, denn sie sind gar nicht so dumm …

Adjective	*Adjektiv*	Eigenschaftswort	**Object**	*Objekt*	Satzergänzung
Adverb	*Adverb*	Umstandswort	**Past Simple**	einfaches *Präteritum* oder *Imperfekt*	einfache Vergangenheit
Adverbiale	Satzerweiterung	Adverbial Phrase	**Personal Pronoun**	*Personalpronomen*	persönliches Fürwort
Adverbial Phrase	*Adverbiale*	Satzerweiterung	**Plural**	Plural	Mehrzahl
Article	*Artikel*	Geschlechtswort	**Possessive Pronoun**	*Possessivpronomen*	besitzanzeigendes Fürwort
Auxiliary	*Hilfsverb*	Hilfszeitwort	*Prädikat*	Satzaussage	Predicate
Bindewort	Conjunction	*Konjunktion*	*Präposition*	Verhältniswort	Preposition
Comparison	*Komparativ*	Vergleich	*Präsens*: einfaches *P.*	einfache Gegenwart	Present Simple
Conjunction	*Konjunktion*	Bindewort	*Präteritum*: einfaches *P.*	einfache Vergangenheit	Past Simple
Demonstrative Pronoun	*Demonstrativpronomen*	hinweisendes Fürwort	**Predicate**	*Prädikat*	Satzaussage
Eigenschaftswort	Adjective	*Adjektiv*	**Preposition**	*Präposition*	Verhältniswort
Einzahl	Singular	*Singular*	**Present Progressive**	– – –	Verlaufsform der Gegenwart
feminin	weiblich	feminine	**Present Simple**	einfaches *Präsens*	einfache Gegenwart
feminine	*feminin*	weiblich	*Pronomen*	Fürwort	Pronoun
Fragefürwort	Interrogative Pronoun	*Interrogativpronomen*	**Pronoun**	*Pronomen*	Fürwort
Fragesatz	Question	– – –	**Question**	– – –	Fragesatz
Fürwort	Pronoun	*Pronomen*	*sächlich*	*neuter*	Neutrum
Fürwort: besitzanzeigendes F.	Possessive Pronoun	*Possessivpronomen*	**Satz**	Sentence	– – –
Fürwort: hinweisendes F.	Demonstrative Pronoun	*Demonstrativpronomen*	**Satzaussage**	Predicate	*Prädikat*
Fürwort: persönliches F.	Personal Pronoun	*Personalpronomen*	**Satzergänzung**	Object	*Objekt*
Future	*Futur*	Zukunft	**Satzbau**	Word order	– – –
Gegenwart: einfache G.	Present Simple	einfaches *Präsens*	**Satzerweiterung**	Adverbial Phrase	*Adverbiale*
Gerund	*Gerundium*	„ing-Form"	**Satzgegenstand**	Subject	*Subjekt*
Geschlechtswort	Article	*Artikel*	**Sentence**	– – –	Satz
Grundform	Infinitive	*Infinitiv*	**Singular**	*Singular*	Einzahl
Hauptwort	Noun	*Substantiv* oder *Nomen*	**Subject**	*Subjekt*	Satzgegenstand
Hilfs*verb*	Hilfszeitwort	Auxiliary	*Substantiv* oder *Nomen*	Hauptwort	Noun
Hilfszeitwort	Auxiliary	Hilfs*verb*	**Umstandswort**	Adverb	*Adverb*
Infinitive	*Infinitiv*	Grundform	**Verb**	*Verb*	Zeitwort
„ing-Form"	Gerund	*Gerundium*	**Vergangenheit: einfache V.**	Past Simple	einfaches *Präteritum* oder *Imperfekt*
Interrogative Pronoun	*Interrogativpronomen*	Fragefürwort	**Vergleich**	Comparison	*Komparativ*
Komparativ	Vergleich	Comparison	**Verhältniswort**	Preposition	*Präposition*
Konjunktion	Bindewort	Conjunction	**Verlaufsform der Gegenwart**	Present Progressive	– – –
männlich	masculine	*maskulin*	**weiblich**	feminine	*feminin*
masculine	*maskulin*	männlich	**Word Order**	– – –	Wortfolge / Satzbau
maskulin	männlich	masculine	**Wortfolge/Satzbau**	Word Order	– – –
Mehrzahl	Plural	*Plural*	**Zeitwort**	Verb	*Verb*
Neuter	*neutrum*	sächlich	**Zukunft**	Future	*Futur*
Neutrum	sächlich	neuter			
Nomen oder **Substantiv**	Hauptwort	Noun			
Noun	*Substantiv* oder *Nomen*	Hauptwort			

Bereich Verb

Grammar

Bereich Verb

1. Auxiliary Verbs / Hilfsverben / Hilfszeitwörter – BE, HAVE, CAN und DO

a) Bildung von BE, HAVE, CAN und DO

be (*sein*)

I	**am**	(I'm)	*ich*	*bin*
you	**are**	(you're)	*du*	*bist/Sie sind*
he	**is**	(he's)	*er*	*ist*
she	**is**	(she's)	*sie*	*ist*
it	**is**	(it's)	*es*	*ist*
we	**are**	(we're)	*wir*	*sind*
you	**are**	(you're)	*ihr*	*seid/Sie sind*
they	**are**	(they're)	*sie*	*sind*

➤ Intro, S. 2, 6, 11, 14, 16

be und **have** haben auch Kurzformen. Diese findest du vor allem im gesprochenen Englisch, seltener im geschriebenen.

have (got) (*haben*)

I	**have**	(got)	(I've got)	*ich habe*
you	**have**	(got)	(you've got)	*du hast/Sie haben*
he	**has**	(got)	(he's got)	*er hat*
she	**has**	(got)	(she's got)	*sie hat*
it	**has**	(got)	(it's got)	*es hat*
we	**have**	(got)	(we've got)	*wir haben*
you	**have**	(got)	(you've got)	*ihr habt/Sie haben*
they	**have**	(got)	(they've got)	*sie haben*

➤ Unit 1, S. 22   ➤ Unit 2, S. 31

have in Verbindung mit **got** bedeutet *haben, besitzen.* Bei **have got** bleibt **got** immer gleich.
have wird zu **has** bei **he/she/it**.
(→ Vergleiche auch Nr. 2, S. 123)

can (*können, dürfen*)

I	**can**	*ich kann/darf*
you	**can**	*du kannst/darfst*
he	**can**	*er kann/darf*
she	**can**	*sie kann/darf*
it	**can**	*es kann/darf*
we	**can**	*wir können/dürfen*
you	**can**	*ihr könnt/dürft*
they	**can**	*sie können/dürfen*

➤ Unit 3, S. 41   ➤ Unit 4, S. 52

do (*tun*)

I	**do**	*ich 'tue'*
you	**do**	*du 'tust'*
he	**does**	*er 'tut'*
she	**does**	*sie 'tut'*
it	**does**	*es 'tut'*
we	**do**	*wir 'tun'*
you	**do**	*ihr 'tut'*
they	**do**	*sie 'tun'*

➤ Unit 8, S. 92

can und **do** haben keine Kurzformen.
can verändert sich nie.

do wird zu **does** bei **he/she/it**.
(→ zum **-s** bei **he/she/it** vergleiche auch Nr. 3, S. 124)

⚠ Aussprache von **does**: [dʌz].

Grammar

Bereich Verb

b) Verneinung von BE, HAVE, CAN und DO: Langform

be

I	am	**not**	
you	are	**not**	
he	is	**not**	
she	is	**not**	
it	is	**not**	
we	are	**not**	
you	are	**not**	
they	are	**not**	

Ich bin nicht....

➤ Intro, S. 16

have got

	have	**not**	got
	have	**not**	got
	has	**not**	got
	has	**not**	got
	has	**not**	got
	have	**not**	got
	have	**not**	got
	have	**not**	got

Ich habe nicht/kein....

➤ Unit 2, S. 31

Um **be, have, can** und **do** zu verneinen, fügst du nur **not** (*nicht, kein*) hinzu.

can

I	**cannot**
you	**cannot**
he	**cannot**
she	**cannot**
it	**cannot**
we	**cannot**
you	**cannot**
they	**cannot**

Ich kann nicht....

➤ Unit 4, S. 52

do

	do	**not**
	do	**not**
	does	**not**
	does	**not**
	does	**not**
	do	**not**
	do	**not**
	do	**not**

Ich tue nicht....

➤ Unit 8, S. 92

⚠ Bei **can** schreibt man das **not** mit **can** zu einem Wort zusammen.

c) Verneinung von BE, HAVE, CAN und DO: Kurzform

	be	have	can	do
I	am not	haven't got	can't	don't
you	aren't	haven't got	can't	don't
he	isn't	hasn't got	can't	doesn't
she	isn't	hasn't got	can't	doesn't
it	isn't	hasn't got	can't	doesn't
we	aren't	haven't got	can't	don't
you	aren't	haven't got	can't	don't
they	aren't	haven't got	can't	don't

➤ Intro, S. 6, 14, 16 ➤ Unit 2, S. 31 ➤ Unit 4, S. 52 ➤ Unit 8, S. 92
➤ Unit 9, S. 108

not wird zu **n't**. Diese Kurzform wird immer mit der Form von **be, have, can** und **do** als ein Wort zusammengeschrieben.

⚠ Bei **I am (I'm)** kann man das **not** nicht verkürzen.

Bei **can** fällt in der verkürzten Verneinung eins der beiden **-n-** weg.

Bereich Verb
Grammar

2. The Present Simple / Das einfache Präsens / Die einfache Gegenwart

a) Die Bildung des Present Simple

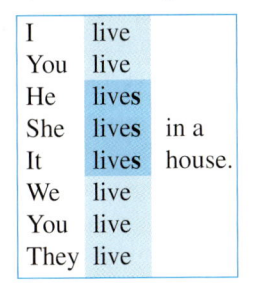

I	live	
You	live	
He	lives	
She	lives	in a
It	lives	house.
We	live	
You	live	
They	live	

I	speak	
You	speak	
He	speaks	
She	speaks	English.
It	speaks	
We	speak	
You	speak	
They	speak	

Für die Bildung des Present Simple musst du dir eins merken: Bei **he/she/it** wird ein **-s** an die Grundform angehängt.

*HE, SHE, IT – Das **S** muss mit!*

➤ Unit 7, S. 83

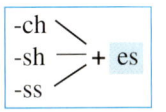

to watch	–	he watches
to wash	–	he washes
to miss	–	he misses

-ch
-sh + es
-ss

Aussprache: [ɪz]

Bei manchen Verben kommt noch ein **-e-** zwischen Grundform und **he/she/it -s**:
- wenn die Grundform auf einen Zischlaut (**-ch, -x, -ss, -sh**) endet;
- bei **do** und **go**.

Aussprache:
| to do | – | he does | [dʌz] |
| to go | – | he goes | [gəʊz] |

➤ Unit 6, S. 74

b) Die Verneinung des Present Simple

I **don't** live in a house.
He **doesn't** speak English.

Die Verneinung wird mit Formen von to do gebildet (siehe S. 129, 2c)

3. The Present Progressive / Die Verlaufsform der Gegenwart (-ing-Form)

a) Die Bildung des Present Progressive

	be	**+**	Grundform	**ing**	
I	am	(I'm)	eat**ing**	a banana.	
You	are	(You're)	help**ing**	me.	
He	is	(He's)	do**ing**	his homework.	
She	is	(She's)	do**ing**	her homework.	
It	is	(It's)	rain**ing**.	(*Es regnet.*)	
We	are	(We're)	play**ing**	cards.	
You	are	(You're)	watch**ing**	TV.	
They	are	(they're)	look**ing**	at the house.	

Das Present Progressive bildest du aus:
1. einer Form von **be** (**am/are/is**);
2. der Grundform des Verbs mit einem angehängten **-ing**.

➤ Unit 4, S. 52

b) Die Verneinung des Present Progressive

	be	**+**	**not**	**+**	Grundform	**ing**	
I	am	**not**	('m **not**)	eating.			
You	are	**not**	(are**n't**)	helping	me.		
He	is	**not**	(is**n't**)	doing	his homework.		
She	is	**not**	(is**n't**)	doing	her homework.		
It	is	**not**	(is**n't**)	raining.			
We	are	**not**	(are**n't**)	playing	cards.		
You	are	**not**	(are**n't**)	watching	TV.		
They	are	**not**	(are**n't**)	looking	at the house.		

Bei der Verneinung tritt **not** (oder **n't**) zwischen **be**-Form (**am/is/are**) und **-ing**-Form.

Grammar

Bereich Verb

c) Schreibregeln für das Present Progressive

make – making
have – having
come – coming
give – giving
live – living

-e → -~~e~~ing

Wenn die Grundform ein **-e** am Ende hat, das man nicht mitspricht, dann verschwindet dieses bei der Bildung der **ing**-Form.

forget – forgetting
sit – sitting
run – running
shop – shopping
stop – stopping

-t → -tting
-n → -nning
-p → -pping

Ein einfacher Mitlaut (z. B. **p, t, n**) am Ende der Grundform wird bei der **-ing**-Form verdoppelt, wenn ein Selbstlaut davor steht (**a, e, i, o, u**), der kurz und betont ist.

4. Wie du Present Progressive und einfaches Präsens gebrauchst

Present Simple: I usually **watch** TV on Thursdays.

Present Progressive: I can't help you now: **I'm** watch**ing** TV.

▶ Unit 4, S. 52

Das Present Simple verwendest du, wenn man etwas normalerweise, immer oder regelmäßig macht. Deswegen steht bei Häufigkeitsangaben das Present Simple.

Das Present Progressive zeigt an, was sich gerade jetzt, in diesem Augenblick abspielt.

5. The will-Future / Das will-Futur / Die Zukunft

I**'ll** come at four o'clock.
I **will** come
I **won't** come to your house.

▶ Unit 3, S. 41

Das will-Futur wird für Voraussagen, Angebote und Versprechen benutzt. Es ist für alle Personen gleich. **Will** wird in der gesprochenen Sprache meistens als **'ll** abgekürzt. Die verneinte Form ist **won't** (= will + not).

6. The Past Simple / Das einfache Präteritum / Die einfache Vergangenheit

a) Die regelmäßige Form des Simple Past

The crow ask**ed** the fox a question.
The mother shout**ed**.

▶ Unit 9, S. 111

An die Grundform des Zeitwortes wird **-ed** angehängt.

b) Die unregelmäßige Form des Simple Past

The fox **ran** into the wood.
The crow **said**, "Good."

▶ Unit 9, S. 111

Wie im Deutschen gibt es keine einfachen Regeln für die Bildung dieser Formen. Du lernst sie einfach. Auf Seite 111 findest du einige aufgelistet.

Bereich Nomen

Grammar

Bereich Nomen

1. The Noun / Das Nomen / Das Hauptwort

a) Singular and Plural / Singular und Plural / Einzahl und Mehrzahl – Bildung und Schreibung

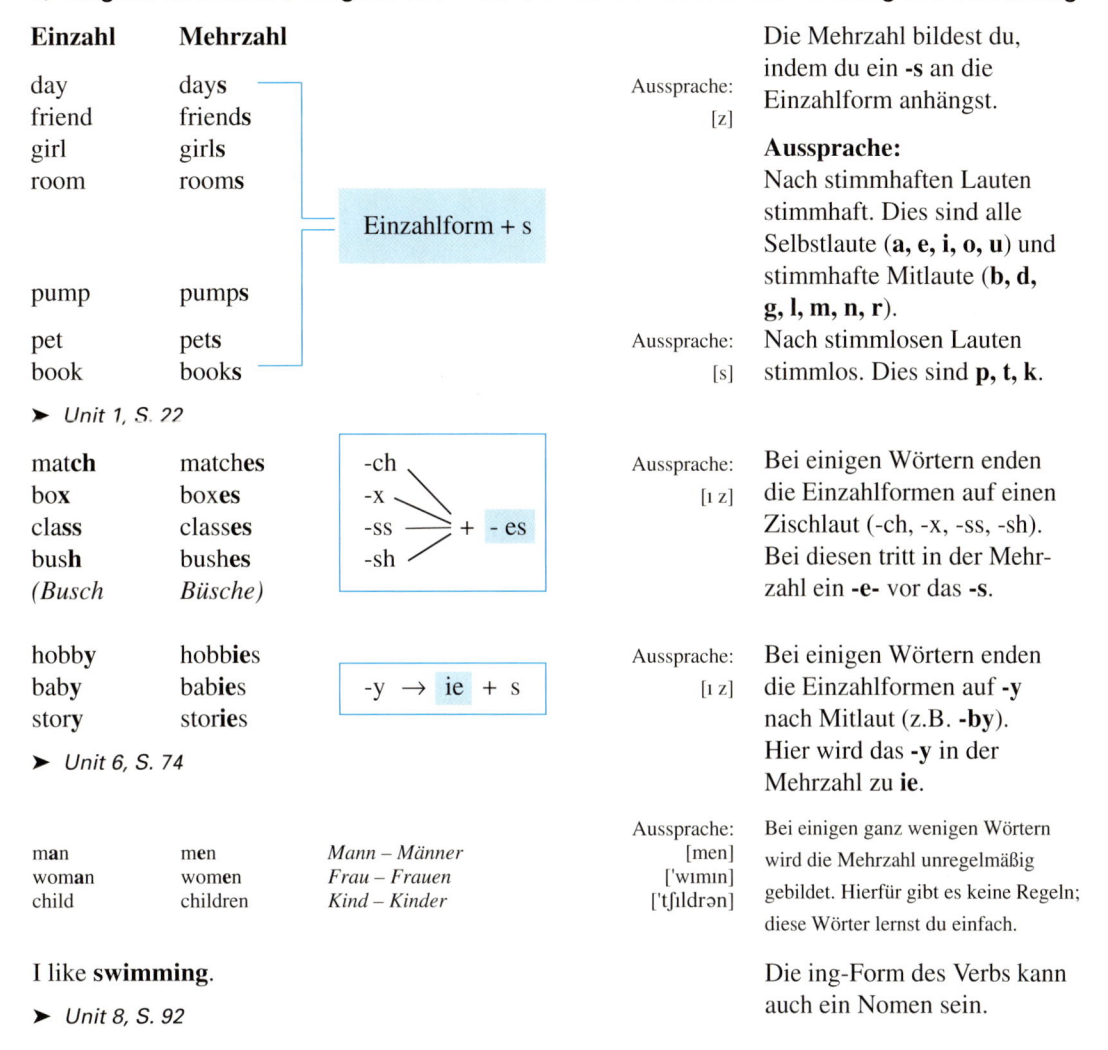

Einzahl	Mehrzahl
day	days
friend	friends
girl	girls
room	rooms
pump	pumps
pet	pets
book	books

Einzahlform + s

Aussprache: [z]

Die Mehrzahl bildest du, indem du ein **-s** an die Einzahlform anhängst.

Aussprache:
Nach stimmhaften Lauten stimmhaft. Dies sind alle Selbstlaute (**a, e, i, o, u**) und stimmhafte Mitlaute (**b, d, g, l, m, n, r**).

Aussprache: [s]

Nach stimmlosen Lauten stimmlos. Dies sind **p, t, k**.

➤ *Unit 1, S. 22*

match	matches
box	boxes
class	classes
bush	bushes
(Busch	*Büsche)*

-ch, -x, -ss, -sh + **-es**

Aussprache: [ɪz]

Bei einigen Wörtern enden die Einzahlformen auf einen Zischlaut (-ch, -x, -ss, -sh). Bei diesen tritt in der Mehrzahl ein **-e-** vor das **-s**.

hobby	hobbies
baby	babies
story	stories

-y → **ie** + s

Aussprache: [ɪz]

Bei einigen Wörtern enden die Einzahlformen auf **-y** nach Mitlaut (z.B. **-by**). Hier wird das **-y** in der Mehrzahl zu **ie**.

➤ *Unit 6, S. 74*

man	men	*Mann – Männer*	
woman	women	*Frau – Frauen*	
child	children	*Kind – Kinder*	

Aussprache: [men] [ˈwɪmɪn] [ˈtʃɪldrən]

Bei einigen ganz wenigen Wörtern wird die Mehrzahl unregelmäßig gebildet. Hierfür gibt es keine Regeln; diese Wörter lernst du einfach.

I like **swimming**.

Die ing-Form des Verbs kann auch ein Nomen sein.

➤ *Unit 8, S. 92*

b) The Genitive-'s / Das Genitiv-'s / Die Besitzform des Hauptwortes mit 's

Mr Christian is Len**'s** monkey. – *Mr Christian ist Lens Affe.*
This is Mark**'s** computer. – *Dies ist Marks Computer.*

's

➤ *Unit 3, S. 41*   ➤ *Unit 6, S. 74*

Die Besitzform wird, wie im Deutschen, mit einem s gebildet.

Das **s** wird durch Apostroph vom Wort getrennt: **'s**.

c) The of-Genitive / Der of-Genitiv / Die Besitzform des Hauptwortes mit of

Paulsgrove is a part **of** Portsmouth.
What's the colour **of** your bike?

➤ *Unit 3, S. 41*

Die Besitzform bei Gegenständen ist meistens **of**.

one hundred and twenty-five 125

Grammar

Bereich Nomen

2. The Article / Der Artikel / Das Geschlechtswort

a) The Indefinite Article / Der unbestimmte Artikel / Das unbestimmte Geschlechtswort

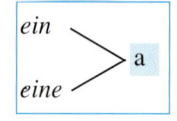

a boy	*ein Junge*		Aussprache:	Männliche, sächliche und
a book	*ein Buch*	ein ⟩ a	[ə]	weibliche Formen, wie im
a cassette	*eine Cassette*	eine ⟩		Deutschen (*ein, eine*), gibt es im Englischen nicht.

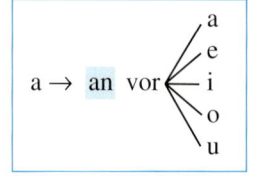

a book	**an** arm		Aussprache:	Vor Wörtern, die mit den
a friend	**an** eye		[ən]	Selbstlauten **a, e, i, o, u** an-
a blue car	**an** Italian boy	a → **an** vor		fangen, wird ein **-n** an den
a new stereo	**an** old stereo	a, e, i, o, u		unbestimmten Artikel ange-
a man	**an** uncle			hängt. Dadurch kannst du Artikel und Wort leichter zusammen aussprechen.

➤ Unit 1, S. 22

b) The Definite Article / Der bestimmte Artikel / Das bestimmte Geschlechtswort

The film is good.
The lady is nice.
The car is fantastic!

The films are good.
The ladies are nice.
The cars are fantastic!

der
die (Einzahl)
das → **the**

die (Mehrzahl)

Aussprache:
[ðə]

Das Englische hat nur einen einzigen bestimmten Artikel. Männliche, weibliche und sächliche Formen gibt es nicht, ebensowenig eine Unterscheidung zwischen Einzahl und Mehrzahl. Es heißt immer **the**.

➤ Intro, S. 6   ➤ Unit 1, S. 22

the	**a**pple
the	**e**gg
the	**i**ll boy
the	**o**ld lady
the	**u**ncle

Aussprache: [ði:]

Steht **the** vor einem Wort, das mit Selbstlaut (**a, e, i, o, u**) anfängt, spricht man es [ði:] aus.

3. The Adjective / Das Adjektiv / Das Eigenschaftswort

a) Einfacher Gebrauch und Form

Paulsgrove is a	**new**	part of Portsmouth.
Len is an	**old**	seaman.
Mr Wilson is	**nice**.	
My sister is	**awful**!	

Das Adjektiv beschreibt eine Person oder Sache näher.

➤ Unit 1, S. 21   ➤ Unit 8, S. 86

We've got an	**old** house. –	… *ein*	*altes Haus.*
Miss Green is an	**old** lady. –	… *eine*	*alte Dame.*
Len is an	**old** man. –	… *ein*	*alter Mann.*

Anders als im Deutschen, haben Adjektive im Englischen immer die gleiche Form.

b) The Comparison / Die Steigerung mit -er / -est

small small**er** small**est**
big big**ger** big**gest**

➤ Unit 3, S. 41   ➤ Unit 9, S. 108

Einsilbige Adjektive werden mit **-er** und **-est** gesteigert. Bei einigen Adjektiven wird der letzte Buchstabe verdoppelt.

Bereich Nomen

Grammar

4. Pronouns / Pronomen / Fürwörter

a) Personal Pronouns / Personalpronomen / Persönliche Fürwörter

Subjektform

I	'm fine.	*ich*
You	're fine.	*du*
He	's fine.	*er*
She	's nice.	*sie*
It	's good.	*es*
We	're all fine.	*wir*
You	're nice.	*ihr*
They	're fine.	*sie*

Objektform

Please visit/help	**me**.	*mich/mir*
Pat visits/helps	**you**.	*dich/dir*
John visits/helps	**him**.	*ihn/ihm*
Kim visits/helps	**her**.	*sie/ihr*
We like/help	**it**.	*es/ihm*
Please visit/help	**us**.	*uns*
Alan visits/helps	**you**.	*euch*
Grant visits/helps	**them**.	*sie/ihnen*

Anders als im Deutschen hat das Englische nur eine Form im Objekt.

➤ Intro, S. 2, 11, 14, 16   ➤ Unit 5, S. 64

b) Possessive Pronouns / Possessivpronomen / Besitzanzeigende Fürwörter

männlich, sächlich / weiblich:

(I)	**my**	dad/mum	*mein Vater / meine Mutter*
(you)	**your**	pen/stereo	*dein Füller / deine Stereoanlage*
(he)	**his**	friend/sister	*sein Freund / seine Schwester*
(she)	**her**	name/class	*ihr Name / ihre Klasse*
(it)	**its**	eye /colour	*sein Auge / seine Farbe*
(we)	**our**	car/school	*unser Auto / unsere Schule*
(you)	**your**	computer/mum	*euer Computer / eure Mutter*
(they)	**their**	house/class	*ihr Haus / ihre Klasse*

Das Possessivpronomen hat keine Unterscheidung zwischen männlich, sächlich und weiblich, oder Einzahl und Mehrzahl, wie im Deutschen.

		Mehrzahl:
my	sisters	*meine Schwestern*
your	friends	*deine Freunde*
her	brothers	*ihre Brüder*
its	colours	*seine Farben*
our	cars	*unsere Autos*
your	computer games	*eure Computer-Spiele*
their	houses	*ihre Häuser*

➤ Intro, S. 2, 11   ➤ Unit 2, S. 31

⚠ Verwechsle nie das Possessivpronomen **its** mit der verkürzten Form **it's** aus **it is** oder **it has**!!! (vergleiche Verbteil: Nr. 1(a), S. 121)

Its colour is green.	–	***Seine** Farbe ist grün.*
It's got a green colour.	–	***Es hat** eine grüne Farbe.*
It's green.	–	***Es ist** grün.*

Grammar

Bereich Satz

c) Demonstrative Pronouns / Demonstrativpronomen / Hinweisende Fürwörter

THAT — **That** isn't my bike.
THIS — **This** is my bike.

Der Unterschied zwischen **this** und **that** liegt in der Entfernung, die du zu dem Gegenstand hast, auf den du hinweist.

➤ Intro, S. 4, 6

5. Prepositions / Präpositionen / Verhältniswörter

over, on, under, behind

Die Präpositionen **on** (auf), **under** (unter), **in** (in), **behind** (hinter), **over** (über) antworten auf die Frage WO?. Deshalb nennt man sie auch Präpositionen des Ortes.

➤ Units 1, 3, 4, 7, 8

Die Wortfolge im Satz

1. Die einfache Aussage

Silvia	*spielt*	*Volleyball.*
Der neue Schüler	*geht*	*in den Judo-Club.*
Silvia	plays	volleyball.
The new pupil	goes	to the judo club.
I	am	in class 5 E.
Grant	is eating	a banana.
You	can have	my bike.
The judo club	is	at the sports centre.

Die Grund-Reihenfolge der Satzglieder im Englischen ist:

Subjekt – Prädikat – Objekt.

Subjekt   **P**rädikat   **O**bjekt

Wer? Was?   Was tut/macht …?   Wen? Was?

S–P–O macht mich froh!

➤ Unit 1, ff.

Bereich Satz

Grammar

2. Der verneinte Satz

a) Verneinte Sätze mit BE

Ich bin nicht in Klasse 5E.

I am **not** in class 5E.
Mr Christian is **not** Grant's monkey.

(I'm not in class 5E.)
(Mr Christian isn't Grant's monkey.)

Subjekt	BE (am/is/are)	NOT	Satzergänzung

Verneinte Sätze mit **be** haben die gleiche Wortfolge wie im Deutschen: Das **not** (**n't**) steht hinter der **be**-Form (**am/is/are**).

(→ Vergleiche auch Nr. 3(b) und 3(c), S.130)

➤ *Intro, S. 6*

b) Verneinte Sätze mit CAN und HAVE

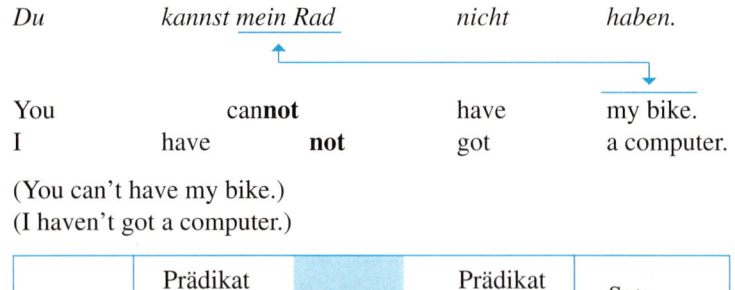

Du kannst mein Rad nicht haben.

You can**not** have my bike.
I have **not** got a computer.

(You can't have my bike.)
(I haven't got a computer.)

Subjekt	Prädikat 1. Teil (Hilfsverb)	NOT	Prädikat 2. Teil (Verb)	Satz-ergänzung

In einem verneinten Satz mit **have (got)** und **can** steht **not** zwischen dem ersten und dem zweiten Teil des Prädikats.

(→ Vergleiche auch Nr. 3(b) und 3(c))

➤ *Unit 2, S. 31*   ➤ *Unit 4, S. 52*

c) Verneinte Sätze o h n e BE, HAVE und CAN

Grant isst keine Bananen.

Grant **does** not eat bananas.
Silvia **does** not play volleyball.
We **do** not like computers.

(Grant doesn't eat bananas.)
(Silvia doesn't play volleyball.)

Subjekt	Prädikat 1. Teil (DO)	NOT	Prädikat 2. Teil (Verb)	Satz-ergänzung

Enthält das Prädikat keine Form von **be**, **can**, **have**, dann fügst du stattdessen **do/does** ein.

➤ *Unit 9, S. 108*

Grammar

Bereich Satz

3. Der Fragesatz

a) Fragesätze mit BE

Bist du der neue Schüler?
Are you the new pupil?
Is Grant Len's friend?

| Prädikat (= BE) | Subjekt | Satzergänzung |

In Fragen steht die **be**-Form (**am/is/are**) am Satzanfang, vor dem Subjekt.

▶ Intro, S. 2, 3, 14, 16

b) Fragesätze mit CAN und HAVE

Kann ich in den Club gehen?

Can I go to the club?
Have you got a computer?

| Prädikat 1. Teil (= CAN, HAVE) | Subjekt | Prädikat 2. Teil (= Verb) | Satzergänzung |

Auch **can** und **have** stehen vor dem Subjekt. Der zweite Teil des Prädikats (Verb) steht zwischen Subjekt und Satzergänzung.

▶ Unit 2, S. 31   ▶ Unit 4, S. 52

Frage nie ohne can, have, do und be!

c) Fragesätze o h n e BE, CAN und HAVE

Does	Grant	eat	bananas?
Does	Silvia	play	volleyball?
Do	you	like	your new teacher?

Ist im Satz keine Form von **be, can** oder **have** vorhanden, so musst du als Ersatz das Hilfsverb **do/does** vorstellen.
⚠ Wenn man **does** hat (**he/she/it**), darf das Verb kein **-s** haben!

▶ Unit 8, S. 92   ▶ Unit 9, S. 108

Bereich Satz

Grammar

d) Fragesätze mit Fragepronomen

Die Fragepronomen **Who**, **What**, **Where**, **When** fragen nach:

Who	is			the small girl?	
What	have	you	got		in your bag?
Where	can	I	sit down?		
When	is	it?			

WER?	– Person
WAS?	– Sache
WO?	– Ort
WANN?	– Zeit

Frage-wort	Prädikat 1. Teil	Subjekt	Prädikat 2. Teil	Satzergänzung

▶ Intro, S. 2, 6, 8

Das Fragewort steht, wie im Deutschen, am Satzanfang. Gleich darauf folgen die Formen von **be**, **have** oder **can**.

Auch hier gilt: Wenn es keine Form von **be**, **can** oder **have** im Satz gibt, mußt du als Ersatz das Verb **do/does** einfügen.

Where	do	they	live?	
What	do	they	eat?	
When	does	Len	work	in his garden?

Frage-wort	Prädikat 1. Teil	Subjekt	Prädikat 2. Teil	Satzergänzung

▶ Unit 9, S. 108

What colour	has	it got?	*Welche* Farbe...?
What films	do	you like?	*Welche* Filme...?

Das Fragepronomen **What** kannst du in Verbindung mit einem Nomen verwenden. Es bedeutet dann: *welche*.

How	much	is this?	*Wie viel...?*
How	many	have you got?	*Wie viele...?*
How	old	is your sister?	*Wie alt...?*

▶ Unit 2, S. 31   ▶ Unit 7, S. 83

Das Fragepronomen **How** steht häufig zusammen mit einem Adjektiv und bedeutet dasselbe wie im Deutschen: *wie* und wird genauso verwendet.

4. Sätze mit Häufigkeits- und Zeitangaben

a) Sätze mit Häufigkeitsangaben mit BE, CAN und HAVE

Grant and John	**are**	always		at Len's house.
Len	**is**	often		in the garden.
I	**can**	sometimes	watch	TV in his house.

Subjekt	Prädikat 1.Teil (Hilfsverb)	Häufig-keits-angabe	Prädikat 2.Teil (Verb)	Satzergänzung

Häufigkeitsangaben wie **often**, **always** usw. stehen zwischen der Form von **be**, **can**, **have** und dem Verb oder der Satzerweiterung.

▶ Unit 6, S. 74

Grammar

Bereich Verb

b) Sätze mit Häufigkeitsangaben o h n e BE, CAN und HAVE

Len	**often**	**watches**	TV.
John	**always**	**plays**	squash.
Kim	**sometimes**	**goes**	to the Club.

Subjekt	Häufig-keits-angabe	Prädikat (Verb)	Satzergänzung

Bei Sätzen ohne Formen von **be**, **can**, **have** stehen die Häufigkeitsangaben vor dem Verb.

➤ *Unit 6, S. 74*

c) Sätze mit Zeitangaben

Len	watches	TV	every **evening**.
Kim	plays	squash	on **Thursdays**.

Subjekt	Prädikat	Objekt	Zeitangaben
		– Satzergänzung –	

Zeitangaben (**evening, Thursday** usw.) stehen am Ende des Satzes.

➤ *Unit 6, S. 74*

d) Sätze mit Zeit- und Ortsangaben

Len	works	in his garden	every **afternoon**.
The boys	are	in Len's house	every **day**.

Subjekt	Prädikat	Orts-angabe	Zeitangaben
		– Satzergänzung –	
		Wo?	Wann? Wie oft?

Bei Sätzen mit Orts- und Häufigkeits- oder Zeitangaben gibt es eine wichtige Regel:

Ort steht vor Zeit!

Ort steht vor Zeit!

➤ *Unit 6, S. 74*

Vocabulary

Hier findest du ein Verzeichnis aller englischen Wörter und Wendungen, die du in diesem Schuljahr lernst. Die Vokabeln erscheinen in derselben Reihenfolge, wie sie vorne im Buch vorkommen. (Alle Namen von Orten, Ländern, Personen usw. kannst du im *Fact Finder* ab S. 165 nachschlagen.)

In der linken Spalte steht jeweils das englische Wort oder die Wendung und dahinter in eckigen Klammern die Aussprache. – Die Aussprachezeichen lernst du in den *Let's-say-it*-Übungen der einzelnen Units. In der mittleren Spalte findest du die deutsche Entsprechung, und in der rechten Spalte stehen weitere Sätze, in denen die wichtigen Wörter im Zusammenhang verwendet werden.

Die **fett gedruckten** Wörter und Wendungen musst du im Gespräch verwenden können. Sie müssen deshalb sehr sorgfältig gelernt werden. Die Wörter im Normaldruck sollst du auf jeden Fall wieder erkennen und verstehen. *Schräg gedruckte* Wörter brauchst du nicht extra zu lernen, da sie nur momentan wichtig sind. Damit du aber auch hier die richtige Aussprache und Bedeutung kennen lernst, haben wir sie ebenfalls aufgenommen.

Aber wie lernt man eigentlich Wörter?

Manche Leute behaupten, man bräuchte sich das Buch nur abends unter das Kopfkissen zu legen. Wir halten diese Methode für sehr unsicher. Versuche es doch einfach mal so:

1 Schaue dir das englische Wort einige Sekunden lang an.
2 Schließe dann die Augen und versuche, dich zu erinnern, wer dieses Wort sagte und bei welcher Gelegenheit das war.
3 Schaue dir das Wort erneut an und sprich es dir dreimal laut vor.
4 Schreibe besonders schwierige Wörter zusätzlich auf einen Zettel.
5 Versuche nun, auf die deutsche Entsprechung zu kommen. Wenn du unsicher bist, schaue einfach in der mittleren Spalte nach.
6 In der rechten Spalte siehst du dann, wie man die wichtigen Wörter im Satzzusammenhang verwendet.

Wir wünschen dir viel Erfolg beim Wörter lernen!

Intro

1	intro(duction) [ˌɪntrə(ˈdʌkʃn)]	*die* Einleitung
	new [njuː]	neu
	friend [frend]	*der/die* Freund(in)
	English [ˈɪŋglɪʃ]	englisch(e, er, es)
	word [wɜːd]	*das* Wort
	camping [ˈkæmpɪŋ]	*das* Zelten, *das* Campen
	CD (compact disc) [siːˈdiː (ˌkəmpækt ˈdɪsk)]	*die* CD
	crash [kræʃ]	*der* Crash
	film [fɪlm]	*der* Film
	farm [fɑːm]	*die* Farm, *der* Bauernhof
	hit [hɪt]	*der* Hit
	hotdog [ˈhɒtdɒg]	*der* Hotdog
	jeans *(Mz*)* [dʒiːnz]	*die* Jeans
	news *(Mz)* [njuːz]	*die* Nachrichten
	recycling [rɪˈsaɪklɪŋ]	*das* Recycling
	shop [ʃɒp]	*der* Laden, *das* Geschäft
	sound [saʊnd]	*der* Laut, *der* Klang
	sport [spɔːt]	*der* Sport
	computer [kəmˈpjuːtə]	*der* Computer
	to start [stɑːt]	anfangen

* *Mz* = Mehrzahl

Vocabulary

Intro

to stop [stɒp]	aufhören	**Stop!**
team [tiːm]	*die* Mannschaft, *das* Team	
to test [test]	prüfen, testen	

Step 1

step [step]	*der* Schritt	
hello! [həˈləʊ]	hallo!, guten Tag!	**Hello**, Pat!
what? [wɒt]	was?	
what's …? [wɒts]	was ist …?	
your [jɔː]	dein(e), Ihr(e)	
name [neɪm]	*der* Name	
what's your name? [ˌwɒts jɔː ˈneɪm]	wie ist dein/Ihr Name?, wie heißt du?, wie heißen Sie?	**What's your name?** – Alec!
and [ænd, ənd]	und	**And** what's your name?
I [aɪ]	ich	
I'm [aɪm]	ich bin	**I'm** Pat.
now [naʊ]	jetzt	**Now** you.
you [juː]	du, Sie	

Step 2

2

good [gʊd]	gut	
morning [ˈmɔːnɪŋ]	*der* Morgen	
good morning! [gʊd ˈmɔːnɪŋ]	guten Morgen!	**Good morning**, Alec!
Mr [ˈmɪstə]	Herr *(Anrede)*	Good morning, **Mr** Wilson.
my [maɪ]	mein(e)	
my name is [ˈmaɪ ˈneɪm ɪz]	mein Name ist, ich heiße	**My name is** Silvia.
Miss [mɪs]	Fräulein *(Anrede)*	I'm **Miss** Green.
you [juː]	du, Sie, ihr	
you are [jʊ ˈɑː]	du bist, Sie sind	**You are** my friend.
Mrs [ˈmɪsɪz]	Frau *(Anrede für verheiratete Frauen)*	Hello, I'm **Mrs** Dean.
yes [jes]	ja	
I am [aɪ ˈæm]	ich bin	Are you Ann Dean? – Yes, **I am**.

Step 3

3

oh! [əʊ]	so!, ach!	
no [nəʊ]	nein	
not [nɒt]	nicht	
I'm not English [aɪm ˌnɒt ˈɪŋglɪʃ]	ich bin kein Engländer/keine Engländerin	Are you English? – No, **I'm not English**.
Scottish [ˈskɒtɪʃ]	*der* Schotte, *die* Schottin; schottisch(e, er, es)	I'm **Scottish**.
American [əˈmerɪkən]	*der* Amerikaner, *die* Amerikanerin; amerikanisch(e, er, es)	You're **American**.
Turkish [ˈtɜːkɪʃ]	*der* Türke, *die* Türkin; türkisch(e, er, es)	Alec is not **Turkish**.
Italian [ɪˈtæljən]	*der* Italiener, *die* Italienerin; italienisch(e, er, es)	Are you **Italian**?

Intro — Vocabulary

German ['dʒɜːmən]	*der* Deutsche, *die* Deutsche; deutsch(e, er, es)	I'm **German**.
Greek [griːk]	*der* Grieche, *die* Griechin; griechisch(e, er, es)	Pat is not **Greek**.
to ask [ɑːsk]	fragen	**Ask** Peter!
to answer ['ɑːnsə]	antworten	Ask and **answer**!
to say [seɪ]	sagen	
let's say it [lets 'seɪ ɪt]	lass(t) es uns sagen	

Step 4

4
how? [haʊ]	wie?	
how are you? [haʊ ˈɑː ju:]	wie geht es dir/Ihnen?	**How are you**, Silvia?
I'm fine [aɪm ˈfaɪn]	mir geht es gut/ausgezeichnet	
thanks [θæŋks]	danke	How are you? – I'm fine, **thanks**.
this [ðɪs]	diese(r, s); das	**This** is Alec.
sister ['sɪstə]	*die* Schwester	This is my **sister**.
what are they saying? [ˌwɒt ɑː ðeɪ ˈseɪɪŋ]	was sagen sie?	
to listen to [ˈlɪsn tə]	hören (auf), zuhören	**Listen to** Pat!
song [sɒŋ]	*das* Lied	
to sing [sɪŋ]	singen	
today [təˈdeɪ]	heute	

Step 5

5
who? [huː]	wer?	
who's? [huːz]	wer ist?	
that [ðæt]	der, die, das (da); jene(r, s)	Who's **that**?
he [hiː]	er	
he's [hiːz]	er ist	**He's** Scottish.
nice [naɪs]	nett	He's **nice**.
that's [ðæts]	das ist	
she [ʃiː]	sie	
she's [ʃiːz]	sie ist	**She's** German.
the [ðə]	der, die, das	
teacher [ˈtiːtʃə]	*der/die* Lehrer(in)	Mrs Dean is the **teacher**.
English teacher [ˈɪŋglɪʃ ˌtiːtʃə]	*der/die* Englischlehrer(in)	
okay [əʊˈkeɪ]	in Ordnung	The teacher is **okay**.
she isn't [ʃiː ˈɪznt]	sie ist nicht	**She isn't** nice.
awful [ˈɔːfl]	schrecklich	He's **awful**.
to look at [ˈlʊk ət]	anschauen, ansehen	**Look at** Alec!
picture [ˈpɪktʃə]	*das* Bild	
in [ɪn]	in	
exercise [ˈeksəsaɪz]	*die* Übung	
right [raɪt]	richtig	That's **right**.
wrong [rɒŋ]	falsch	That's **wrong**.
to talk about [ˈtɔːk əˌbaʊt]	sprechen über/von	**Talk about** the film!
people *(Mz)* [ˈpiːpl]	*die* Leute	**People** talk about the French film.

6
please [pliːz]	bitte	
to complete [kəmˈpliːt]	vervollständigen, ergänzen	

Vocabulary

Intro

Step 6

in English [ɪnˈɪŋglɪʃ]	auf Englisch	
boy [bɔɪ]	*der* Junge	Alec is a **boy**.
girl [gɜːl]	*das* Mädchen	Kim is a **girl**.
to come in [kʌmˈɪn]	hereinkommen	**Come in**, boys and girls.
please [pliːz]	bitte	Listen to the song, **please**.
to sit down [sɪtˈdaʊn]	sich (hin)setzen	**Sit down**, please.
now [naʊ]	also, nun	Look at the picture, **now**.
it [ɪt]	es	
it's [ɪts]	es ist	**It's** a nice shop.
a [ə]	ein(e)	Mrs Dean is **a** teacher.
calculator [ˈkælkjʊleɪtə]	*der* Taschenrechner	
to stand up [stændˈʌp]	aufstehen	**Stand up**, now!

7
book [bʊk]	*das* Buch	The **book** is nice.
pen [pen]	*der* Füllfederhalter, *der* Füller	It's a **pen**.
rubber [ˈrʌbə]	*der* Radiergummi	
chair [tʃeə]	*der* Stuhl	What's that in English, please? – It's a **chair**.
table [ˈteɪbl]	*der* Tisch	It's a **table**.
pencil [ˈpensl]	*der* Bleistift	
biro [ˈbaɪrəʊ]	*der* Kugelschreiber	It's a **biro**.
school bag [ˈskuːl bæg]	*die* Schultasche, -mappe	It's my **school bag**.
blackboard [ˈblækbɔːd]	*die* Tafel	
desk [desk]	*der* Schreibtisch	It's my **desk**.
window [ˈwɪndəʊ]	*das* Fenster	What's 'Fenster' in English? – It's a **window**.

8
classroom [ˈklɑːsrʊm]	*das* Klassenzimmer	

Step 7

9
classroom [ˈklɑːsrʊm]	*das* Klassenzimmer	The boys and girls are in the **classroom**.
mum [mʌm]	*die* Mutter, *die* Mutti	Who's that? – That's my **mum**.
very [ˈverɪ]	sehr	My desk is **very** small.
small [smɔːl]	klein	The German teacher is very **small**.
her [hɜː]	ihr(e)	That's **her** book.
his [hɪz]	sein(e)	That's **his** biro.
bag [bæg]	*die* Tasche	The **bag** is very nice.

10 **partner** [ˈpɑːtnə] — *der/die* Partner(in) — You're my **partner**.
11 **to make** [meɪk] — machen — **Make** a list.
list [lɪst]	*die* Liste	
you're [jʊə]	du bist	**You're** okay.

Step 8

sorry! [ˈsɒrɪ]	Entschuldigung!, Verzeihung!	**Sorry**, Mr Wilson!
dad [dæd]	*der* Vater, *der* Vati	My **dad** is nice.
house [haʊs]	*das* Haus	Our **house** is small.
big [bɪg]	groß	My bag is **big**.
what about …? [ˈwɒt əˌbaʊt]	was ist mit …?, wie steht es mit …?	**What about** your friend?
here [hɪə]	hier, da	Is your mum **here**?

Intro / Unit 1 — Vocabulary

Step 9

13 we [wiː] — wir
   we're [wɪə] — wir sind — **We're** Kim and Pat.
   you [juː] — dir, dich/euch, euch/Ihnen, Sie — What about **you**?
   we aren't [wiːˌˈɑːnt] — wir sind nicht/keine — **We aren't** English.

Step 10

15 they [ðeɪ] — sie *(Mz)*
   they're [ˈðeə] — sie sind — **They're** small.
16 talk [tɔːk] — *das* Gespräch

Tasks

17 task [tɑːsk] — *die* Aufgabe
   quiz [kwɪz] — *das* Quiz
   cassette [kəˈset] — *die* Kassette
   clown [klaʊn] — *der* Clown
   professor [prəˈfesə] — *der* Professor
   telephone [ˈtelɪfəʊn] — *das* Telefon — That's a **telephone**.
   question [ˈkwestʃən] — *die* Frage — Answer my **question**, please.
   or [ɔː] — oder
   to act [ækt] — darstellen, mimen
   scene [siːn] — *die* Szene

Unit 1

18 unit [ˈjuːnɪt] — *die* Lektion
   in [ɪn] — in — We're **in** Portsmouth.
   around [əˈraʊnd] — um … (herum)
   British [ˈbrɪtɪʃ] — *der* Brite, *die* Britin; britisch(e, er, es)
   port [pɔːt] — *der* Hafen
   part [pɑːt] — *der* Teil — Paulsgrove is a **part** of Portsmouth.
   of [ɒv, əv] — von — This is a part **of** Portsmouth.
   castle [ˈkɑːsl] — *die* Burg, *das* Schloss
   street [striːt] — *die* Straße — Castle **Street** is in Portsmouth.
   an [ən] — ein(e) — This is **an** exercise.
   old [əʊld] — alt — Portchester is very **old**.
   town [taʊn] — *die* Stadt — Portsmouth is a big **town**.
   near [nɪə] — in der Nähe von, nahe bei — Portchester is **near** Portsmouth.

A

19 bighead [ˈbɪghed] — *der/die* Angeber(in)
   at home [æt ˈhəʊm] — zu Hause — My father is **at home**.
   room [ruːm (rʊm)] — *das* Zimmer — This is my **room**.
   I've got [aɪv ˈɡɒt] — ich habe — **I've got** a nice teacher.
   computer [kəmˈpjuːtə] — *der* Computer — I've got a **computer**.
   have you got? [hæv juː ˈɡɒt] — hast du? — **Have you got** a nice cassette? – No, I haven't.

Vocabulary   Unit 1

eight [eɪt]	acht	I've got **eight** friends.
game [ɡeɪm]	*das* Spiel	I've got a computer **game**.
great [ɡreɪt]	großartig	Computers are **great**.
our [ˈaʊə]	unser(e, er, es)	**Our** cassettes are awful.
television [ˈtelɪvɪʒn]	*der* Fernseher	My **television** is new.
we've got [wiːv ˈɡɒt]	wir haben	**We've got** a television.
stereo [ˈsterɪəʊ]	*die* Stereoanlage	Our **stereo** is new.
hundred [ˈhʌndrɪd]	hundert	
video [ˈvɪdɪəʊ]	*das* Video(gerät)	Our **video** is great.
car [kɑː]	*das* Auto	That's an old **car**.
two [tuː]	zwei	I've got **two** school bags.
goodbye! [ɡʊdˈbaɪ]	auf Wiedersehen!	**Goodbye**, Miss Green!
20 **what's missing?** [wɒts ˈmɪsɪŋ]	was fehlt?	
to say [seɪ]	sagen	**Say** 'Fernseher' in English!
number [ˈnʌmbə]	*die* Zahl, *die* Nummer	Eight is a **number**.
one [wʌn]	eins	You've got **one** car.
three [θriː]	drei	Have you got **three** rubbers?
four [fɔː]	vier	I've got **four** sisters.
five [faɪv]	fünf	We've got **five** chairs.
six [sɪks]	sechs	You've got **six** biros.
seven [ˈsevn]	sieben	Four and three is **seven**.
nine [naɪn]	neun	We've got **nine** cassettes.
ten [ten]	zehn	I've got **ten** books.
eleven [ɪˈlevn]	elf	**Eleven** is a number.
twelve [twelv]	zwölf	I've got **twelve** pencils.

B

21 **family** [ˈfæməlɪ]	*die* Familie	
telephone number [ˈtelɪfəʊn ˌnʌmbə]	*die* Telefonnummer	
together [təˈɡeðə]	zusammen, miteinander	

D

23 **again** [əˈɡen]	noch einmal, wieder	Let's say 'television' **again**.
it's your turn [ɪts ˈjɔː tɜːn]	du bist an der Reihe	
rhyme [raɪm]	*der* Reim, *der* Vers	
to close [kləʊz]	zumachen	**Close** the window, please.
door [dɔː]	*die* Tür	
late [leɪt]	(zu) spät	

Time for revision

24 **time** [taɪm]	*die* Zeit	
for [fɔː]	für	I've got time **for** you.
revision [rɪˈvɪʒn]	*die* Wiederholung	
class [klɑːs]	*die* Klasse	Alec is in our **class**.
25 **to write about** [ˈraɪt əˌbaʊt]	schreiben über	**Write about** the book.
to take [teɪk]	nehmen	**Take** the book.
piece [piːs]	*das* Stück	

Unit 1 / 2

Vocabulary

paper ['peɪpə]	*das* Papier	
a piece of paper [ˌpiːs ə v 'peɪpə]	ein Blatt Papier, ein Zettel	
to stick [stɪk]	anheften, kleben	
photo(graph) ['fəʊtəʊ ('fəʊtəɡrɑːf)]	*das* Foto	
on [ɒn]	auf	The photo is **on** the piece of paper.
mother ['mʌðə]	*die* Mutter	My **mother** is German.
father ['fɑːðə]	*der* Vater	My **father** is German.
brother ['brʌðə]	*der* Bruder	Bill is my **brother**.
cousin ['kʌzn]	*der* Cousin, *die* Cousine	
aunt [ɑːnt]	*die* Tante	
uncle ['ʌŋkl]	*der* Onkel	
too [tuː]	auch	My aunt is Italian, **too**.

Unit 2

26

problem ['prɒbləm]	*das* Problem	I've got a big **problem**.
oh no! [əʊ 'nəʊ]	ach du Schande!	
their [ðeə]	ihr(e) *(Mz)*	It's **their** pump.
bike [baɪk]	*das* Fahrrad	The boy is on his **bike**.
they've got [ðeɪv 'ɡɒt]	sie haben	**They've got** a calculator.
pump [pʌmp]	*die* (Luft-)Pumpe	They haven't got a **pump**.

A

hey! [heɪ]	he!, heda!	
you've got [juːv 'ɡɒt]	du hast	**You've got** a bike.
flat [flæt]	platt	
tyre ['taɪə]	*der* Reifen	
flat tyre [flæt 'taɪə]	*die* Reifenpanne, *der* Platten	
he has got [ˌhiː həz 'ɡɒt]	er hat	**He has got** a flat tyre.
he hasn't got [ˌhiː hæznt 'ɡɒt]	er hat nicht/kein(e, en)	**He hasn't got** a pump.
to get [ɡet]	holen	**Get** the book, please!
dog [dɒɡ]	*der* Hund	Skipper is a nice **dog**.

27

monkey ['mʌŋkɪ]	*der* Affe	Mr Christian is a **monkey**.
how old? [haʊ 'əʊld]	wie alt?	**How old** is your sister?
teatime ['tiːtaɪm]	*die* Teestunde	
tea [tiː]	*der* Tee	**Tea** is good.
cup [kʌp]	*die* Tasse	My mum has got twelve **cups**.
cupboard ['kʌbəd]	*der* (Küchen-)Schrank	The cups are in the **cupboard**.
how many? [haʊ 'menɪ]	wie viele?	**How many** cups are in the cupboard?
milk [mɪlk]	*die* Milch	**Milk** in tea is good.
sugar ['ʃʊɡə]	*der* Zucker	The **sugar** is on the table.
pet [pet]	*das* Haustier	Skipper is a **pet**.
clever ['klevə]	klug, schlau	Monkeys are **clever**.
man *(Mz:* **men)** [mæn (men)]	*der* Mann	Len is an old **man**.

Vocabulary

Unit 2

B

29 handbag ['hændbæg] — *die* Handtasche
   club [klʌb] — *der* Club — Paulsgrove has got a video **club**.

30 riddle ['rɪdl] — *das* Rätsel
   giraffe [dʒɪ'rɑːf] — *die* Giraffe
   to pass [pɑːs] — vorbeigehen

D

32 concertina [kɒnsə'tiːnə] — *die* Ziehharmonika
   fisherman ['fɪʃəmən] — *der* Fischer
   ship [ʃɪp] — *das* Schiff
   bottle ['bɒtl] — *die* Flasche — The **bottle** is on the table.
   tin [tɪn] — *die* Büchse, *die* Dose — The tea is in the **tin** on the table.

   worm [wɜːm] — *der* Wurm
   sweets *(Mz)* [swiːts] — *die* Süßigkeiten — **Sweets** are nice.
   we shall [ʃæl] — wir sollen
   to do [duː] — tun, machen
   with [wɪð] — mit
   sailor ['seɪlə] — *der* Matrose, *der* Seemann
   early ['ɜːlɪ] — früh
   in the morning [ɪn ðə 'mɔːnɪŋ] — am Morgen

   to rise up [raɪz ʌp] — sich aufbäumen
   him [hɪm] — ihn
   till [tɪl] — bis
   traditional [trə'dɪʃənəl] — traditionell, überliefert

33 **magazine** [mægə'ziːn] — *die* Zeitschrift — The **magazine** is awful.
   to read [riːd] — lesen — Let's **read** the school magazine!

   article ['ɑːtɪkl] — *der* Artikel
   thing [θɪŋ] — *das* Ding, *die* Sache — Len has got great **things** in his house.

   but [bʌt] — aber — Grant is English, **but** Alec isn't.
   some [sʌm] — etwas
   help [help] — *die* Hilfe

Time for activities

34 activities *(Mz)* [æk'tɪvətɪz] — *die* Aktivitäten, *die* Unternehmungen

   picture ['pɪktʃə] — *das* Bild — The **pictures** are nice.
   in the picture [ɪn ðə 'pɪktʃə] — auf dem Bild
   to play [pleɪ] — spielen
   pocket ['pɒkɪt] — *die* Tasche *(an Kleidungsstücken)*

   difference ['dɪfrəns] — *der* Unterschied
   where? [weə] — wo? — **Where** is Alec?
   where's? [weəz] — wo ist?

Unit 3

35 afternoon [ɑːftəˈnuːn] — *der* Nachmittag
evening [ˈiːvnɪŋ] — *der* Abend
time [taɪm] — *die* Zeit — They haven't got **time**.
what's the time? [ˌwɒts ðə ˈtaɪm] — wie viel Uhr ist es? — **What's the time**, please?
past [pɑːst] — nach — It's ten **past** two.
half past seven [ˌhɑːf pɑːst ˈsevn] — halb acht — It's **half past seven**.
it's ... o'clock [ɪts ... əˈklɒk] — es ist ... Uhr — **It's** eight **o'clock**.

A

36 closed [ˈkləʊzd] — geschlossen — Is your shop **closed**?
open [ˈəʊpən] — geöffnet — No, it's **open** till eight o'clock.
I can't [aɪ ˈkɑːnt] — ich kann nicht
to find [faɪnd] — finden — I can't **find** my new school bag. – Where is it?
her [hɜː] — sie *(persönl. Fürwort, Einzahl)* — Where is Miss Green? Can you look for **her**?
piano lesson [pɪˈænəʊ ˌlesən] — *die* Klavierstunde
maybe [ˈmeɪbɪ] — vielleicht
park [pɑːk] — *der* Park
to look for [ˈlʊk fə] — suchen — I can't find my book. Can you **look for** it?
we'll [wiːl] — wir werden — **We'll** find it.
thank you [ˈθæŋk jʊ] — danke — Can you give me the pencil, please? – **Thank you**.
there [ðeə] — dort, da — **There** she is.
hi! [haɪ] — hallo!
seagull [ˈsiːɡʌl] — *die* Seemöwe
hurt [hɜːt] — verletzt
really [ˈrɪəlɪ] — wirklich
its [ɪts] — ihr(e), sein(e) *(sächlich)* — This is a house. **Its** windows are small.
leg [leɡ] — *das* Bein — Birds have got two **legs**.
broken [ˈbrəʊkən] — gebrochen
to help [help] — helfen
soon [suːn] — bald — Please write **soon**.
let's go [lets ˈɡəʊ] — lass(t) uns gehen, gehen wir — **Let's go** to school.
to go [ɡəʊ] — gehen — Kim and John **go** to school.
together [təˈɡeðə] — zusammen, miteinander — Let's go **together**.
37 woman (*Mz:* women) [ˈwʊmən (ˈwɪmɪn)] — *die* Frau — Miss Green is a **woman**.
bird [bɜːd] — *der* Vogel — A seagull is a big **bird**.
oh dear! [ˈəʊ dɪə] — oh je!
to be [biː, bɪ] — sein — I'll **be** at Len's house at six o'clock.
we're on our way [wɪə ˌɒn ˌaʊə ˈweɪ] — wir sind auf dem Weg
a lot of [ə ˈlɒt ˌəv] — viele
animal [ˈænɪml] — *das* Tier — Dogs and seagulls are **animals**.
bigger [ˈbɪɡə] — größer

Vocabulary   Unit 3

than [ðæn, ðən]	als *(Vergleich)*	
smaller ['smɔ:lə]	kleiner	
tired ['taɪəd]	müde	
hungry ['hʌŋgrɪ]	hungrig	
to give [gɪv]	geben	**Give** me the book, please.
fish [fɪʃ]	der/die Fisch(e)	Len will give it a **fish**.
to put [pʊt]	setzen, legen	
garden ['gɑ:dn]	der Garten	
to stay [steɪ]	bleiben	
he won't [hɪ 'wəʊnt]	er wird nicht	
to fly away [flaɪ‿ə'weɪ]	wegfliegen	
to watch [wɒtʃ]	beobachten, ansehen	Let's **watch** the bird.

B _____

39 cold [kəʊld]   kalt
    warm [wɔ:m]   warm
    hot [hɒt]   heiß
40 swimming pool ['swɪmɪŋ ˌpu:l]   das Schwimmbad, -becken
    video shop ['vɪdɪəʊ ˌʃɒp]   das Videogeschäft

D _____

42 **to** [tʊ]   zu(m)   They take the bird **to** Len's house.

    to burn [bɜ:n]   brennen
    to fetch [fetʃ]   holen
    fire ['faɪə]   das Feuer
    water ['wɔ:tə]   das Wasser
43 bed [bed]   das Bett

Time for activities

44 to draw [drɔ:]   zeichnen
    eye [aɪ]   das Auge
    mouth [maʊθ]   der Mund
    nose [nəʊz]   die Nase
    to show [ʃəʊ]   zeigen
    drawing ['drɔ:ɪŋ]   die Zeichnung
    funny ['fʌnɪ]   lustig
    wall [wɔ:l]   die Wand
    to guess [ges]   raten
45 poster ['pəʊstə]   das Poster, das Plakat
    newspaper ['nju:speɪpə]   die Zeitung   Peter is reading the **newspaper**.
    Christmas ['krɪsməs]   Weihnachten   **Christmas** is nice.
    card [kɑ:d]   die Karte
    tree [tri:]   der Baum
    happy ['hæpɪ]   froh   He's very **happy**.
    merry ['merɪ]   fröhlich
    year [jɪə]   das Jahr
    from [frɒm, frəm] von   The Christmas card is **from** Alec.

Vocabulary

Unit 3 / 4

Christmas carol ['krɪsməs 'kærəl]	*das* Weihnachtslied	
to wish [wɪʃ]	wünschen	

Unit 4

46
fun [fʌn]	*der* Spaß	This game is **fun**.
centre ['sentə]	*das* Zentrum, *das* Center	Ann is going to the sports **centre**.
to play [pleɪ]	spielen	Can you **play** tennis?
squash [skwɒʃ]	Squash	**Squash** is great.
volleyball ['vɒlibɔːl]	Volleyball	Peter is playing **volleyball**.
football ['fʊtbɔːl]	Fußball	**Football** is a great game.
basketball ['bɑːskɪtbɔːl]	Basketball	Let's play **basketball**!
tennis ['tenɪs]	Tennis	Silvia is playing **tennis**.
judo ['dʒuːdəʊ]	Judo	**Judo** is boring.
free [friː]	kostenlos	

A

47
where? [weə]	wohin?	**Where** is he going?
there is [ðeər ɪz]	es gibt, da ist	**There is** a monkey in the garden.
there's [ðeəz]	es gibt, da ist	Look, **there's** George!
at [æt]	in	There's a club **at** the Mountbatten Centre.
swimming ['swɪmɪŋ]	*das* Schwimmen	Alec is going **swimming**.
swimming pool ['swɪmɪŋ ˌpuːl]	*das* Schwimmbad, -becken	There is a **swimming pool** at the club.
what a pity! [wɒt ə 'pɪti]	wie schade!	
good at ['gʊd æt]	gut (in)	He's **good at** judo.
all right [ɔːl 'raɪt]	ganz gut, in Ordnung	
bad [bæd]	schlecht, schlimm	Sweets are **bad** for you.
not bad at [nɒt 'bæd æt]	nicht schlecht in	He's **not bad at** tennis.
can [kæn, kən]	können	I **can** wash the car.
not really [nɒt 'rɪəli]	eigentlich nicht	Are you good at tennis? – **Not really**.
judo is fun [ˌdʒuːdəʊ ɪz 'fʌn]	Judo macht Spaß	
idea [aɪ'dɪə]	*die* Idee, *der* Einfall	
with [wɪð]	mit	Len is in his house **with** his dog and his monkey.
us [ʌs]	uns	We have got a flat tyre. Please help **us**.
I can't (cannot) [aɪ 'kɑːnt ('kænnɒt)]	ich kann nicht	**I can't** play squash.
homework ['həʊmwɜːk]	*die* Hausaufgabe(n)	He's doing his **homework**.

48
there are [ðeər ɑː]	es gibt, da sind	**There are** two swimming pools at the sports centre.
only ['əʊnli]	nur	
dangerous ['deɪndʒərəs]	gefährlich	
expensive [ɪk'spensɪv]	teuer	
well [wel]	also	

Vocabulary

Unit 4

B

49	electrical shop [ɪˌlektrɪkl 'ʃɒp]	das Elektrogeschäft	
	television (TV) ['telɪvɪʒn (tiː'viː)]	der Fernsehapparat	
	clock [klɒk]	die (Stand-, Wand)Uhr	
	bed [bed]	das Bett	I go to **bed** in the evening.
51	to phone [fəʊn]	anrufen, telefonieren	
	to watch TV [ˌwɒtʃ tiː'viː]	fernsehen	Kim is **watching TV**.
	music ['mjuːzɪk]	die Musik	They listen to the **music**.
	to open ['əʊpən]	öffnen	

D

53	welcome to ['welkəm tə]	willkommen in/im	
	fantastic [fæn'tæstɪk]	fantastisch	
	bye! [baɪ]	*umgangssprachlich:* wiedersehen!, tschüs!	
	to do [duː]	tun, machen	What are you **doing**?
	survey ['sɜːveɪ]	die Umfrage	
	group [gruːp]	die Gruppe	That's your **group**.
	like this [laɪk 'ðɪs]	so, folgendermaßen	

Time for a story

54	story ['stɔːrɪ]	die Geschichte	
	to sit [sɪt]	sitzen	
	box [bɒks]	die Schachtel, die Kiste	
	nut [nʌt]	die Nuss	
	a box of nuts [ə ˌbɒks əv 'nʌts]	eine Schachtel Nüsse	
	summer ['sʌmə]	der Sommer	
	day [deɪ]	der Tag	It's a nice summer **day**.
	village ['vɪlɪdʒ]	das Dorf	
	the village of Crickwood [ðə ˌvɪlɪdʒ əv 'krɪkwʊd]	das Dorf Crickwood	
	hamster ['hæmstə]	der Hamster	
	wonderful ['wʌndəfʊl]	wunderbar	
	into ['ɪntʊ]	in … hinein	He's going from the garden **into** the house.
	kitchen ['kɪtʃɪn]	die Küche	
	field [fiːld]	das Feld	
	in the fields [ɪn ðə 'fiːldz]	auf den Feldern	
	to get into [get 'ɪntə]	hineinkommen	
	let me … ['let miː]	lass mich …	
	to think [θɪŋk]	nachdenken, überlegen	
	key [kiː]	der Schlüssel	
	always ['ɔːlweɪz]	immer	You're awful. You're **always** late.
	under ['ʌndə]	unter	
	doormat ['dɔːmæt]	der Fußabstreifer	
	lock [lɒk]	das Schloss	
	then [ðen]	dann, also	
	to hang [hæŋ]	hängen	

Unit 4
Vocabulary

to open [ˈəʊpən]	öffnen, aufmachen	**Open** the door, please.
to run [rʌn]	rennen, laufen	
easy [ˈiːzɪ]	einfach	
pond [pɒnd]	*der* Teich	
to eat [iːt]	essen	My sister is **eating** a hamburger.
full [fʊl]	voll	
heavy [ˈhevɪ]	schwer	
to drop [drɒp]	fallen lassen	
grass [grɑːs]	*das* Gras	
to see [siː]	sehen	I can **see** a monkey in the garden.
quick [kwɪk]	schnell	

Magazine 1

Cinema food?

55 *cinema* [ˈsɪnəmə]   *das* Kino
food [fuːd]   *das* Essen
favourite [ˈfeɪvərɪt]   Lieblings-
popcorn [ˈpɒpkɔːn]   *das* Popcorn
bucket [ˈbʌkɪt]   *der* Eimer
a bag of sweets [ə ˈbæg əv ˈswiːts]   eine Tüte Süßigkeiten
cheaper [ˈtʃiːpə]   billiger
kiosk [ˈkiːɒsk]   *der* Kiosk
ice cream [ˈaɪs ˌkriːm]   *das* Eis
bestseller [ˈbestselə]   *der* Bestseller
to like [laɪk]   mögen
cake [keɪk]   *der* Kuchen
cola [ˈkəʊlə]   *die* Cola
birthday [ˈbɜːθdeɪ]   *der* Geburtstag
breakfast [ˈbrekfəst]   *das* Frühstück
cornflakes [ˈkɔːnfleɪks]   *die* Cornflakes
apple [ˈæpl]   *der* Apfel
banana [bəˈnɑːnə]   *die* Banane
crisps [krɪsps]   *die* Chips
fries [fraɪz]   *die* Pommes frites

Great ideas for more pocket money

56 *more* [mɔː]   mehr
money [ˈmʌnɪ]   *das* Geld
grandmother [ˈgrænmʌðə]   *die* Großmutter
neighbour [ˈneɪbə]   *der/die* Nachbar(in)
to go shopping [gəʊ ˈʃɒpɪŋ]   einkaufen gehen
to clean [kliːn]   putzen, sauber machen
to work [wɜːk]   arbeiten
to baby-sit [ˈbeɪbɪsɪt]   babysitten
young children [ˈjʌŋ ˈtʃɪldrən]   kleine Kinder
baby-sitting [ˈbeɪbɪsɪtɪŋ]   *das* Babysitten

Vocabulary Unit 4

kid [kɪd]   *das* Kind
to be asleep [bɪ‿əˈsliːp]   schlafen
a lot of the time [ə ˈlɒt‿əv ðə ˌtaɪm]   die meiste Zeit
to visit [ˈvɪzɪt]   besuchen
them [ðem]   sie *(Mz)*
pound [paʊnd]   *das* Pfund
Sunday [ˈsʌndɪ]   *der* Sonntag
month [mʌnθ]   *der* Monat
to tell [tel]   erzählen, sagen
board [bɔːd]   *die* Tafel

Halloween

57   *last* [lɑːst]   letzte(r, s)
day [deɪ]   *der* Tag
October [ɒkˈtəʊbə]   *der* Oktober
before [bɪˈfɔː]   vor *(zeitlich)*
against [əˈgenst]   gegen
ghost [gəʊst]   *der* Geist, *das* Gespenst
witch (Mz: witches) [wɪtʃ (ˈwɪtʃɪz)]   *die* Hexe
lantern [ˈlæntən]   *die* Laterne
to invite [ɪnˈvaɪt]   einladen
as [æz, əz]   als
monster [ˈmɒnstə]   *das* Monster
custom [ˈkʌstəm]   *der* Brauch
when? [wen]   wann?
pumpkin [ˈpʌmpkɪn]   *der* Kürbis
to cut out [ˈkʌt ˈaʊt]   ausschneiden
middle [ˈmɪdl]   *die* Mitte
face [feɪs]   *das* Gesicht
candle [ˈkændl]   *die* Kerze
harvest festival [ˈhɑːvɪst ˈfestɪvəl]   *das* Erntedankfest
first [fɜːst]   erste(r, s)
colonist [ˈkɒlənɪst]   *der/die* Siedler(in)
was [wɒz, wəz]   war *(Vergangenheit)*
1621 (sixteen hundred and twenty-one) [ˈsɪkstiːn ˈhʌndrəd ənd ˈtwentɪ ˈwʌn]   1621 *(Jahreszahl)*
is called [ɪz ˈkɔːld]   wird genannt
holiday [ˈhɒlɪdeɪ]   *der* Urlaub
fourth [fɔːθ]   vierte(r, s)
Thursday [ˈθɜːzdɪ]   Donnerstag
November [nəʊˈvembə]   *der* November

Silly jokes

58   *silly* [ˈsɪlɪ]   dumm, albern
joke [dʒəʊk]   *der* Witz
to walk [wɔːk]   gehen
a pair of [ə ˈpeər‿əv]   ein Paar

Unit 4 / 5

mouse [maʊs] — *die* Maus
elephant ['elɪfənt] — *der* Elefant
colour ['kʌlə] — *die* Farbe
writing ['raɪtɪŋ] — *die* (Hand-)Schrift
letter ['letə] — *der* Brief

Unit 5

59 **robot** ['rɒbɒt] — *der* Roboter — The **robot** is eating an apple.
to [tʊ] — vor — It's five **to** eight.
a quarter to nine [ə ˌkwɔːtə tʊ] — Viertel vor *neun* — It's **a quarter to** nine.
to sleep [sliːp] — schlafen — The robot is **sleeping**.

A

60 super ['suːpə] — super
to walk [wɔːk] — gehen — The robot can **walk**.
toy [tɔɪ] — *das* Spielzeug
made in ['meɪd ɪn] — hergestellt in
to speak [spiːk] — sprechen — I can **speak** English.
French [frentʃ] — *der* Franzose, *die* Französin; französisch(e, er, es) — He speaks **French**.

to live [lɪv] — wohnen, leben — Alec **lives** in London.
to shut up [ʃʌt ʌp] — ruhig sein, den Mund halten
a cup of tea [ə ˌkʌp əv tiː] — eine Tasse Tee
bonjour! [bõˈʒuːr] — *Französisch:* guten Tag!
chemists ['kemɪsts] — *die* Drogerie
61 chips *(Mz)* [tʃɪps] — *die* Pommes frites
to dance [dɑːns] — tanzen
lady ['leɪdɪ] — *die* Dame — The **lady** is very nice.
to like [laɪk] — mögen, gern haben — The robot **likes** the lady.
him [hɪm] — ihn — She likes **him**, too.
happy ['hæpɪ] — glücklich
in control of [ɪn kənˈtrəʊl əv] — Kontrolle über

thirteen [θɜːˈtiːn] — dreizehn
fourteen [fɔːˈtiːn] — vierzehn
twenty ['twentɪ] — zwanzig
twenty-one [twentɪˈwʌn] — einundzwanzig
thirty ['θɜːtɪ] — dreißig
forty ['fɔːtɪ] — vierzig
fifty ['fɪftɪ] — fünfzig
sixty ['sɪkstɪ] — sechzig
seventy ['sevntɪ] — siebzig
eighty ['eɪtɪ] — achtzig
ninety ['naɪntɪ] — neunzig
a/one hundred ['hʌndrəd] — (ein)hundert

B

62 breakfast ['brekfəst] — *das* Frühstück
banana [bəˈnɑːnə] — *die* Banane — Monkeys like **bananas**.
rain [reɪn] — *der* Regen

Vocabulary

Unit 5 / 6

	umbrella [ʌmˈbrelə]	*der* Regenschirm
63	whoo-hoo! [ˈwuːˈhuː]	Juhu!
	twenty-two oh-two [ˈtwentɪtuː əʊˈtuː]	22 Uhr 02
	shoe [ʃuː]	*der* Schuh
	Odd man out [ˌɒd mænˈaʊt]	*Name eines Spiels (Ein Wort fällt heraus)*
	to forget [fəˈget]	vergessen
64	postman [ˈpəʊstmən]	*der* Postbote, *die* Postbotin; *der/die* Briefträger(in)
	knock [nɒk]	*das* Klopfen
	glad [glæd]	froh
	8.05 (eight oh-five) [ˈeɪt əʊ ˈfaɪv]	8 Uhr 05
	8.30 (eight thirty) [ˈeɪt ˈθɜːtɪ]	8 Uhr 30
	thirty-five [ˈθɜːtɪfaɪv]	fünfunddreißig
	forty-five [ˈfɔːtɪfaɪv]	fünfundvierzig
	to visit [ˈvɪzɪt]	besuchen

Alec has got nice **shoes**.

Grant **visits** his aunt.

D

65	**letter** [ˈletə]	*der* Brief
	reader [ˈriːdə]	*der/die* Leser(in)
	hobby (*Mz:* hobbies) [ˈhɒbɪ (ˈhɒbɪz)]	*das* Hobby
	to work [wɜːk]	arbeiten
	school [skuːl]	*die* Schule
66	**pupil** [ˈpjuːpl]	*der/die* Schüler(in)
	note [nəʊt]	*die* Notiz
	to tell about [ˈtel ə ˌbaʊt]	erzählen von
	person [ˈpɜːsn]	*die* Person

Peter writes a **letter**.

My father **works** at home.
Martin is good at **school**.

Tell me **about** your friend.

Time for revision

67	magic [ˈmædʒɪk]	magisch, Zauber-
	square [skweə]	*das* Quadrat

Unit 6

68	neighbour [ˈneɪbə]	*der/die* Nachbar(in)

A

69	**every** [ˈevrɪ]	jede(r, s)
	to do the shopping [ˌduː ðə ˈʃɒpɪŋ]	Einkäufe machen
	sometimes [ˈsʌmtaɪmz]	manchmal
	often [ˈɒfn]	oft
	Thursday [ˈθɜːzdɪ]	Donnerstag
	on Thursdays [ɒn ˈθɜːzdɪz]	donnerstags

Len is in his garden **every** afternoon.

She **sometimes** does her shopping, too.
Mr Christian **often** helps Len.

She visits her grandmother **on Thursdays**.

Unit 6   Vocabulary

	week [wiːk]	die Woche	
	whose? [huːz]	wessen?	
	what's the matter? [ˌwɒts ðə ˈmætə]	was ist los?	
	funny [ˈfʌnɪ]	komisch	
	today [təˈdeɪ]	heute	Is it Thursday **today**?
70	the leg is bad today [ðə ˌleg ɪz ˈbæd təˈdeɪ]	das Bein ist heute schlimm, es tut besonders weh	
	Saturday [ˈsætədɪ]	Sonnabend, Samstag	Today is **Saturday**.
	shopping day [ˈʃɒpɪŋ deɪ]	der Einkaufstag	
	shopping list [ˈʃɒpɪŋ lɪst]	die Einkaufsliste	
	packet [ˈpækɪt]	die Packung	Ann buys a **packet** of tea.
	a packet of tea [ə ˌpækɪt əv ˈtiː]	eine Packung Tee	
	I'd like [aɪd ˈlaɪk]	ich möchte bitte, ich hätte gern	
	jar [dʒɑː]	das Glas, der Glasbehälter	
	coffee [ˈkɒfɪ]	der Kaffee	
	a jar of coffee [ə ˌdʒɑːr əv ˈkɒfɪ]	ein Glas Kaffee	
	food [fuːd]	das Futter, die Nahrung, die Lebensmittel	People eat a lot of **food**.
	match (*Mz:* **matches**) [mætʃ (ˈmætʃɪz)]	das Streichholz, das Zündholz	**Matches** are dangerous.
	a bag of sugar [ə ˌbæg əv ˈʃʊgə]	eine Tüte Zucker	
71	to learn [lɜːn]	lernen	
	body [ˈbɒdɪ]	der Körper	
	head [hed]	der Kopf	Elephants have got big **heads**.
	to hurt [hɜːt]	wehtun, verletzen	
	eye [aɪ]	das Auge	Dave has got big **eyes**.
	mouth [maʊθ]	der Mund	His **mouth** is very small.
	arm [ɑːm]	der Arm	My **arms** hurt today.
	hand [hænd]	die Hand	My **hands** are big.
	finger [ˈfɪŋgə]	der Finger	A hand has got five **fingers**.
	foot [fʊt]	der Fuß	Peter's **foot** hurts.
	Monday [ˈmʌndɪ]	Montag	
	Tuesday [ˈtjuːzdɪ]	Dienstag	
	Wednesday [ˈwenzdɪ]	Mittwoch	
	Friday [ˈfraɪdɪ]	Freitag	
	Sunday [ˈsʌndɪ]	Sonntag	

D

75	*bingo* [ˈbɪŋgəʊ]	*Name eines Spiels*	
	to wash [wɒʃ]	waschen	My neighbour **washes** his car on Saturdays.
	everybody [ˈevrɪbɒdɪ]	jeder, alle	
	cake [keɪk]	der Kuchen	
	no more [nəʊ mɔː]	keine … mehr	
	biscuit [ˈbɪskɪt]	der/das Keks	
	bread [bred]	das Brot	We buy **bread** today.

Vocabulary

Unit 6 / 7

Time for activities

76	letter ['letə]	der Buchstabe	
	to sell [sel]	verkaufen	Mr Harman **sells** computers.
	sea [siː]	das Meer	
77	*pawn* [pɔːn]	*die* Spielfigur	
	dice [daɪs]	*der* Würfel	
	winner ['wɪnə]	der/die Gewinner(in), der/die Sieger(in)	
	to go on to [gəʊ ˌɒn tə]	weitergehen zu	
	to go back to [gəʊ 'bæk tə]	zurückgehen zu	
	to move [muːv]	ziehen	
	to miss [mɪs]	aussetzen	
	turn [tɜːn]	*die* Runde	

Unit 7

78	**money** ['mʌnɪ]	das Geld	We've got a lot of **money**.
	coin [kɔɪn]	die Münze	
	bank note ['bæŋk nəʊt]	die Banknote, der Geldschein	
	pound (£) [paʊnd]	das Pfund *(brit. Währung)*	I've only got one **pound**.
	penny *(Mz:* pence) (= p) ['penɪ (pens)]	britische Münzeinheit	
	how much is …? [ˌhaʊ 'mʌtʃ ɪz]	wie viel kostet …?	**How much is** the video?
	that's six pounds [ðæts ˌsɪks 'paʊndz]	das kostet/macht sechs Pfund	How much is the book? – **That's six pounds**.

A

79	**really** ['rɪəlɪ]	eigentlich, wirklich	She's **really** nice.
	cigarette [ˌsɪgə'ret]	die Zigarette	
	drink [drɪŋk]	das Getränk	How much are the **drinks**?
	chocolate ['tʃɒklət]	die Schokolade	My sister likes **chocolate**.
	corner shop [ˌkɔːnə 'ʃɒp]	kleiner Laden an der Ecke, „Tante-Emma-Laden"	
	Asian ['eɪʃn]	der Asiate, die Asiatin; asiatisch(e, er, es)	
	parents *(Mz)* ['peərənts]	die Eltern	Your mother and father are your **parents**.
	flat [flæt]	die Wohnung	
	above [ə'bʌv]	über	
	Indian ['ɪndjən]	der Inder, die Inderin; indisch(e, er, es)	
	to love [lʌv]	lieben, gern mögen	
	other ['ʌðə]	andere(r, s)	
	things are fine [ˌθɪŋs ɑː 'faɪn]	alles läuft gut	
	to want [wɒnt]	wollen, wünschen	Skipper **wants** a biscuit.
	one day [wʌn 'deɪ]	eines Tages	
80	all [ɔːl]	alles	
	is that all? [ˌɪz ðæt 'ɔːl]	ist das alles?	**Is that all**? – Yes, thanks.
	here you are [ˌhɪə juː ˈɑː]	bitte schön	That's £ 6.45. – **Here you are**.

Unit 7 / 8   Vocabulary

B _____

82 vegetables *(Mz)* ['vedʒtəblz]   *das* Gemüse   **Vegetables** are good for you.
    I don't know [ˌaɪ dəʊnt   ich weiß nicht
      'nəʊ]

D _____

83 picnic ['pɪknɪk]   *das* Picknick
    teddy bear ['tedɪ beə]   *der* Teddybär
    text [tekst]   *der* Text
    wood [wʊd]   *der* Wald
    honey ['hʌnɪ]   *der* Honig
    little ['lɪtl]   klein(er, es)
    to match [mætʃ]   kombinieren
    sentence ['sentəns]   *der* Satz
84 to go into the greengrocer's   in den Gemüseladen gehen
      [ˌgəʊ ˌɪntə ðə
      'griːngrəʊsəz]
    to go into the newsagent's   zum Zeitungshändler gehen
      [ˌgəʊ ˌɪntə ðə
      'njuːzeɪdʒənts]
    supermarket ['suːpəmɑːkɪt]   *der* Supermarkt
    newsagent ['njuːzeɪdʒənt]   *der* Zeitungshändler
    of course [əv 'kɔːs]   selbstverständlich
    sir [sɜː]   mein Herr *(Anrede)*
    greengrocer ['griːngrəʊsə]   *der* Gemüsehändler
    pardon? ['pɑːdn]   wie bitte?

Time for activities

85 season ['siːzn]   *die* Jahreszeit
    month [mʌnθ]   *der* Monat
    spring [sprɪŋ]   *der* Frühling
    March [mɑːtʃ]   *der* März
    April ['eɪprəl]   *der* April
    May [meɪ]   *der* Mai
    June [dʒuːn]   *der* Juni
    July [dʒʊ'laɪ]   *der* Juli
    August ['ɔːgəst]   *der* August
    autumn ['ɔːtəm]   *der* Herbst
    September [sep'tembə]   *der* September
    October [ɒk'təʊbə]   *der* Oktober
    November [nəʊ'vembə]   *der* November
    winter ['wɪntə]   *der* Winter
    December [dɪ'sembə]   *der* Dezember
    January ['dʒænjʊərɪ]   *der* Januar
    February ['februərɪ]   *der* Februar

Unit 8 _____

86 far [fɑː]   fern
    smart [smɑːt]   schick
    coat [kəʊt]   *der* Mantel   Have you got a smart **coat**?

Vocabulary Unit 8

dress [dres]	*das* Kleid	Pat has got a nice **dress**.
skirt [skɜːt]	*der* Rock	Kim's **skirt** is great!
pullover [ˈpʊləʊvə]	*der* Pullover	
hat [hæt]	*der* Hut	
T-shirt [ˈtiːʃɜːt]	*das* T-Shirt	
blouse [blaʊz]	*die* Bluse	
jacket [ˈdʒækɪt]	*die* Jacke, *das* Jackett	
trousers *(Mz)* [ˈtraʊzəz]	*die* Hose	His **trousers** are smart.
sock [sɒk]	*die* Socke	
cap [kæp]	*die* Kappe, *die* Mütze	
shirt [ʃɜːt]	*das* Hemd	Peter's **shirt** is new.
to wear [weə]	*(Kleidung)* tragen, anhaben	What are you **wearing** today?
opinion [əˈpɪnjən]	*die* Meinung	
uniform [ˈjuːnɪfɔːm]	*die* Uniform	
87 colour [ˈkʌlə]	*die* Farbe	
black [blæk]	schwarz	My trousers are **black**.
brown [braʊn]	braun	
blue [bluː]	blau	Alec's socks are **blue**.
green [griːn]	grün	Kim has got **green** shoes.
yellow [ˈjeləʊ]	gelb	The uniform is **yellow**.
violet [ˈvaɪələt]	violett	
red [red]	rot	Pat has got a **red** dress.
pink [pɪŋk]	pink	
white [waɪt]	weiß	The shirt is **white**.
grey [greɪ]	grau	
what colour is/are …? [ˈwɒt ˈkʌlər‿ɪz/ɑː]	welche Farbe hat/haben …?	

A _____

carnival [ˈkɑːnɪvl]	*der* Karneval, *der* Fasching	
parade [pəˈreɪd]	*die* Parade, *der* Umzug	
next [nekst]	nächste(r, s)	
silly [ˈsɪli]	dumm, albern	
anyway [ˈenɪweɪ]	wie dem auch sei, jedenfalls	
88 photographer [fəˈtɒgrəfə]	*der* Fotograf	
excuse me [ɪkˈskjuːz miː]	entschuldige/entschuldigen Sie, Verzeihung	
way [weɪ]	*der* Weg	Can you tell me the **way**?
to hate [heɪt]	nicht mögen, hassen	
to go down [gəʊ ˈdaʊn]	hinuntergehen	
road [rəʊd]	*die* Straße	The Grove Club is in Marsden **Road**.
traffic lights *(Mz)* [ˈtræfɪk laɪts]	*die* Ampel	
to cross [krɒs]	überqueren	
to turn [tɜːn]	abbiegen	**Turn** right here!
right [raɪt]	rechts	Now turn **right**.
left [left]	links	Now turn **left**.
on the left/right [ɒn ðə ˈleft]	auf der linken/rechten Seite	The club is **on the left**.

Unit 8 Vocabulary

B

90	church [tʃɜːtʃ]		die Kirche
91	station [ˈsteɪʃn]		der Bahnhof
	post office [ˈpəʊst ˌɒfɪs]		das Postamt
	to spell [spel]		buchstabieren
	double [ˈdʌbl]		doppelt, *hier:* zweimal

D

93	grandma [ˈgrænmɑː]		*umgangssprachlich: die* Großmutter, *die* Oma
	flower [ˈflaʊə]		die Blume
	busy [ˈbɪzi]		beschäftigt, geschäftig
	to have a great time [ˌhæv ə ɡreɪt ˈtaɪm]		sich amüsieren, großen Spaß haben
	funfair [ˈfʌnfeə]		der Rummelplatz
	stall [stɔːl]		die Bude
	band [bænd]		die Band
	festival [ˈfestɪvəl]		das Festival, *das* Fest
	before [bɪˈfɔː]		vor *(zeitlich)*
	report [rɪˈpɔːt]		der Bericht
	to lead [liːd]		anführen
	behind [bɪˈhaɪnd]		hinter
	hill [hɪl]		der Hügel
	after [ˈɑːftə]		nach
	to finish [ˈfɪnɪʃ]		aufhören, zu Ende gehen
	to scream [skriːm]		schreien, kreischen
	to put on [pʊt ˈɒn]		anziehen

Time for activities

95	he couldn't [kʊdnt]		er konnte nicht
	to get up [get ˈʌp]		aufstehen
	to go round [gəʊ ˈraʊnd]		(im Kreis) herum gehen
	hand [hænd]		*hier: der* (Uhr)Zeiger
	slow [sləʊ]		langsam
96	sky [skaɪ]		der Himmel
	tongue-twister [ˈtʌŋ ˌtwɪstə]		der Zungenbrecher
	feather [ˈfeðə]		die Feder
	why? [waɪ]		warum?
	long [lɒŋ]		lang
	something [ˈsʌmθɪŋ]		etwas
	to begin [bɪˈgɪn]		anfangen, beginnen
97	message [ˈmesɪdʒ]		die Botschaft
	code [kəʊd]		die Geheimschrift

Magazine 2

Do you watch too much TV?

98	*too* [tuː]		zu
	much [mʌtʃ]		viel

Vocabulary   Unit 8

ad (Abk. f.: advertisement) [æd (əd'vɜːtɪsmənt)]	der Werbespot, die Anzeige
never ['nevə]	nie(mals)
to sing [sɪŋ]	singen
real [rɪəl]	richtig, tatsächlich
star [stɑː]	der Star, die Berühmtheit
favourite ['feɪvərɪt]	Lieblings-
programme ['prəʊgræm]	die Sendung, das Programm
to play [pleɪ]	spielen
to switch off [swɪtʃ 'ɒf]	abschalten, ausschalten
point [pɔɪnt]	der Punkt
normal ['nɔːməl]	normal
whoah! [wəʊ]	Halt!, Stop!
problem ['prɒbləm]	das Problem
you haven't [jʊ 'hævnt]	du hast nicht/ihr habt nicht

Come to the circus!

99
circus ['sɜːkəs]	der Zirkus
youngest ['jʌŋgəst]	jüngste(r, s)
acrobat ['ækrəbæt]	der Akrobat
show [ʃəʊ]	die Show, die Vorführung
kilo ['kɪləʊ]	das Kilo
so [səʊ]	daher, also
bacon ['beɪkən]	der Speck
egg [eg]	das Ei
lunch [lʌntʃ]	das Mittagessen
training ['treɪnɪŋ]	das Training
hour ['aʊə]	die Stunde
private ['praɪvət]	privat, Privat-
trailer (AE) ['treɪlə]	der Wohnwagen
famous ['feɪməs]	berühmt, bekannt
life [laɪf]	das Leben
to climb [klaɪm]	klettern
to dive [daɪv]	tauchen
boxing ['bɒksɪŋ]	das Boxen
acrobatics [ækrə'bætɪks]	die Akrobatik
to have no idea [həv ˌnəʊ aɪ'dɪə]	keine Ahnung haben

Silly jokes

100
drum [drʌm]	die Trommel
in the street [ɪn ðə 'striːt]	auf der Straße
to jump [dʒʌmp]	springen, hüpfen
higher ['haɪə]	höher
wall [wɔːl]	die Mauer
sure [ʃʊə]	sicher
to bring [brɪŋ]	herbringen, holen
potato (Mz: potatoes) [pə'teɪtəʊ (pə'teɪtəʊz)]	die Kartoffel
to get wet [get 'wet]	nass werden
taxi driver ['tæksɪ draɪvə]	der/die Taxifahrer(in)

Unit 8 / 9   Vocabulary

Your letters

101 *gave (to give)* [geɪv (gɪv)] — gab, -st, -en
it's called [ɪts 'kɔːld] — es heißt
saw (to see) [sɔː (siː)] — sah, -st, -en
wanted (to want) ['wɒntɪd (wɒnt)] — wollte, -en, -t
were [wɜː] — warst, -en, -t
had (to have) [hæd (hæv)] — hatte, -st, -en
same [seɪm] — selbe(r, s)
started (to start) ['stɑːtɪd (stɑːt)] — gründete, -st, -en
price [praɪs] — der Preis
ticket ['tɪkɪt] — der Schein, das Ticket
started (to start) [stɑːtɪd (stɑːt)] — begann
visited (to visit) [vɪzɪtɪd (vɪzɪt)] — besuchte
looked (to look) [lʊkd (lʊk)] — schaute, sah
went (to go) [went (ɡəʊ)] — ging

Unit 9

A

103 to ask questions [ˌɑːsk 'kwestʃənz] — Fragen stellen
to come from ['kʌm frəm] — kommen aus/von
originally [əˈrɪdʒənəlɪ] — ursprünglich
ferry (*Mz:* ferries) ['ferɪ ('ferɪz)] — die Fähre
housewife (*Mz:* housewives) ['haʊswaɪf ('haʊswaɪvz)] — die Hausfrau — Alec's mother is a **housewife**.
job [dʒɒb] — der Job, die Stelle — Ann Dean has got a good **job**.
Gaelic ['ɡeɪlɪk, 'ɡælɪk] — gälisch *(schottische Minderheitssprache)*
to know [nəʊ] — kennen, wissen — Mrs Ross **knows** a few Gaelic words.
a few [ə 'fjuː] — ein paar
Scots [skɒts] — die Schotten
bagpipes ['bæɡpaɪps] — der Dudelsack
kilt [kɪlt] — der Kilt, der Schottenrock
when? [wen] — wann? — **When** do you have breakfast?
pub [pʌb] — die Kneipe, das Wirtshaus
subject ['sʌbdʒekt] — das Schulfach
to like best [laɪk 'best] — am liebsten mögen
Maths [mæθs] — Mathe(matik)
favourite ['feɪvərɪt] — liebstes, Lieblings- — Maths is my **favourite** subject.
last [lɑːst] — letzte(r, s)
to miss [mɪs] — vermissen — Do you **miss** Scotland?

Vocabulary   Unit 9

B

104	Drama ['drɑːmə]	Drama, Schauspiel *(Schulfach)*
	Physical Education (= P.E.)	Sport, Turnen *(Schulfach)*
	[ˌfɪzɪkl ˌedjʊˈkeɪʃn (piː iː)]	
	fitness ['fɪtnəs]	Fitness
105	*centipede* ['sentɪpiːd]	*der* Tausendfüßler
	wooden leg [ˌwʊdn ˈleg]	*das* Holzbein
106	lunch [lʌntʃ]	*das* Mittagessen
107	bear [beə]	*der* Bär
	elephant ['elɪfənt]	*der* Elefant — An **elephant** is a big animal.

D

108	timetable ['taɪmˌteɪbl]	*der* Stundenplan
	Art [ɑːt]	Kunst, *der* Kunstunterricht
	Science ['saɪəns]	Naturwissenschaften
	Religious Education (= R.E.)	*der* Religionsunterricht
	[rɪˌlɪdʒəs edjʊˈkeɪʃn (ɑː iː)]	
	Computer Studies	Informatik
	[kəmˈpjuːtə ˌstʌdɪz]	
	break [breɪk]	*die* Pause
109	different ['dɪfrənt]	anders
	interview ['ɪntəvjuː]	*das* Interview
	pop music ['pɒp ˌmjuːzɪk]	*die* Popmusik
	folk music ['fəʊk ˌmjuːzɪk]	*die* Folkmusik
	hamburger ['hæmbɜːgə]	*der* Hamburger

Time for a story

110	crow [krəʊ]	*die* Krähe
	lovely ['lʌvlɪ]	wunderschön, herrlich
	fox [fɒks]	*der* Fuchs
	nest [nest]	*das* Nest
	up [ʌp]	oben
	baby ['beɪbɪ]	*das* Baby
	shouted (to shout) ['ʃaʊtɪd (ʃaʊt)]	rief (-st, -en), schrie (-st, -n)
	to throw down [θrəʊ ˈdaʊn]	herunter werfen
	answered (to answer) ['ɑːnsəd (ˈɑːnsə)]	antwortete (-st, -n) — The pupil **answered** the question.
	to come up [kʌm ˈʌp]	heraufkommen
	I'm afraid [əˈfreɪd]	ich habe Angst
	was [wɒz, wəz]	war *(Vergangenheit)* — The mother bird **was** very afraid.
	also ['ɔːlsəʊ]	auch
	to climb [klaɪm]	klettern
	flew (to fly) [fluː (flaɪ)]	flog (-st, -en)
	angry ['æŋgrɪ]	ärgerlich
	saw (to see) [sɔː (siː)]	sah (-st, -en) — One day the fox **saw** the crow.
	ran away (to run away) [ræn əˈweɪ (rʌn əˈweɪ)]	rannte (-st, -n) weg

Unit 9 / Play — Vocabulary

lay down (to lie down) [leɪ 'daʊn (laɪ 'daʊn)]	legte (-st, -n) sich hin	
ground [graʊnd]	*der* Boden	
closed (to close) [kləʊzd (kləʊz)]	schloss (-est, -en)	
dead [ded]	tot	
thought (to think) [θɔːt (θɪŋk)]	dachte (-st, -n)	
opened (to open) ['əʊpənd ('əʊpən)]	öffnete (-st, -n)	
fool [fuːl]	*der* Dummkopf	
laughed (to laugh) [lɑːfd (lɑːf)]	lachte (-st, -n)	
later ['leɪtə]	später	
plan [plæn]	*der* Plan	
came (to come) [keɪm (kʌm)]	kam (-st, -en)	
still [stɪl]	noch immer	
jumped on to (to jump on to) [dʒʌmpt 'ɒntʊ (dʒʌmp 'ɒntʊ)]	sprang auf	
caught (to catch) [kɔːt (kætʃ)]	fing (-st, -en)	
end [end]	*das* Ende	
dinner ['dɪnə]	*das* Abendessen	
asked (to ask) [ɑːskt (ɑːsk)]	fragte (-st, -n)	The fox **asked**: "Aren't you afraid?"
said (to say) [sed (seɪ)]	sagte (-st, -n)	"Oh yes," **said** the crow. "Please eat me!"
high [haɪ]	hoch	
rock [rɒk]	*der* Fels	
through [θruː]	durch	
fell (to fall) [fel (fɔːl)]	fiel (-st, -en) herunter	

Play

112
ghost [gəʊst]	*der* Geist, *das* Gespenst	
hunter ['hʌntə]	*der* Jäger	
as [æz]	als	
hall [hɔːl]	*das* Herrenhaus, *das* Schloss	

Scene 1

hotel [həʊ'tel]	*das* Hotel	
so [səʊ]	so, also	
midnight ['mɪdnaɪt]	*die* Mitternacht	
at midnight [æt 'mɪdnaɪt]	um Mitternacht	
113	must [mʌst]	müssen	
to wait [weɪt]	warten	
to have got to [hæv 'gɒt tə]	müssen	
brochure ['brəʊʃə]	*die* Broschüre, *der* Katalog	
tourist ['tʊərɪst]	*der* Tourist	A **tourist** usually sleeps in a hotel.
need [niːd]	brauchen	
I see ['aɪ ˌsiː]	(ich) verstehe, ah ja	

Vocabulary   Play

night [naɪt]	*die* Nacht	Ghosts usually come at **night**.
to take a photo [ˌteɪk‿ə ˈfəʊtəʊ]	ein Foto machen	
good night! [gʊd ˈnaɪt]	gute Nacht!	**Good night**, Dave!
madam [ˈmædəm]	gnädige Frau *(Anrede)*	

Scene 2

camera [ˈkæmərə] — *die* Kamera, *der* Fotoapparat
cassette-recorder [kəˈsetrɪˌkɔːdə] — *der* Kassettenrekorder

Scene 4

114 child *(Mz:* children) [tʃaɪld (ˈtʃɪldrən)] — *das* Kind
to happen [ˈhæpən] — passieren
115 because [bɪˈkɔːz] — weil
I'm sorry [aɪm ˈsɒrɪ] — es tut mir leid, Verzeihung
to say hello [seɪ ˈheləʊ] — grüßen, einen Gruß ausrichten
when [wen] — wenn
'night! [naɪt] — *umgangssprachlich:* gute Nacht!

Scene 5

terrible [ˈterəbl] — schrecklich, furchtbar

Wordfields

117 *wordfield* [ˈwɜːdfiːəld] — *das* Wortfeld
feeling [ˈfiːlɪŋ] — *das* Gefühl
118 *clothes (Mz)* [kləʊðz] — *die* Kleidung
119 *to talk* [tɔːk] — sprechen
to sing [sɪŋ] — singen

Dictionary

Wenn du ein Wort nicht mehr weißt, kannst du es in dieser Übersicht nachschlagen. Du findest hier die englischen Wörter und Wendungen in alphabetischer Reihenfolge.

Nach dem englischen Stichwort siehst du seine Aussprache und die deutsche Entsprechung. Wörter, die du lernen musst, sind halbfett gedruckt. Die anderen solltest du verstehen, wenn du sie hörst oder liest.

A

a [ə] ein(e)
above [əˈbʌv] über
act [ækt] darstellen, mimen
activities *(Mz)* [ækˈtɪvətɪz] *die* Aktivitäten, *die* Unternehmungen
afraid [əˈfreɪd]: I'm afraid ich habe Angst
after [ˈɑːftə] nach
afternoon [ˌɑːftəˈnuːn] *der* Nachmittag
again [əˈgen] noch einmal, wieder
all [ɔːl] alles: **is that all?** ist das alles?
always [ˈɔːlweɪz] immer
American [əˈmerɪkən] *der* Amerikaner, *die* Amerikanerin; amerikanisch(e, er, es)
an [ən] ein(e)
and [ænd, ənd] und
angry [ˈæŋgrɪ] ärgerlich
animal [ˈænɪml] *das* Tier
answer [ˈɑːnsə] antworten: **answered** antwortete (-st, -n)
anyway [ˈenɪweɪ] wie dem auch sei, jedenfalls
April [ˈeɪprəl] *der* April
arm [ɑːm] *der* Arm
around [əˈraʊnd] um ... (herum)
Art [ɑːt] Kunst, *der* Kunstunterricht
article [ˈɑːtɪkl] *der* Artikel
as [æz] als
Asian [ˈeɪʃn] *der* Asiate, *die* Asiatin; asiatisch(e, er, es)
ask [ɑːsk] fragen: **asked** fragte (-st, -n)
at [æt] in
August [ˈɔːgəst] *der* August
aunt [ɑːnt] *die* Tante
autumn [ˈɔːtəm] *der* Herbst
awful [ˈɔːfl] schrecklich

B

bad [bæd] schlecht, schlimm: **not bad at** nicht schlecht in; the leg is bad today das Bein ist heute schlimm, es tut besonders weh

bag [bæg] *die* Tasche: a bag of sugar eine Tüte Zucker
bagpipes [ˈbægpaɪps] *der* Dudelsack
banana [bəˈnɑːnə] *die* Banane
band [bænd] *die* Band
bank note [ˈbæŋk nəʊt] *die* Banknote, *der* Geldschein
basketball [ˈbɑːskɪtbɔːl] Basketball
be [biː, bɪ] sein
bear [beə] *der* Bär
because [bɪˈkɒz] weil
bed [bed] *das* Bett
before [bɪˈfɔː] vor *(zeitlich)*
behind [bɪˈhaɪnd] hinter
big [bɪg] groß: bigger größer
bighead [ˈbɪghed] der/die Angeber(in)
bike [baɪk] *das* Fahrrad
bird [bɜːd] *der* Vogel
biro [ˈbaɪrəʊ] *der* Kugelschreiber
biscuit [ˈbɪskɪt] der/das Keks
black [blæk] schwarz
blackboard [ˈblækbɔːd] *die* Tafel
blouse [blaʊz] *die* Bluse
blue [bluː] blau
body [ˈbɒdɪ] *der* Körper
bonjour! [bõˈʒuːr] *Französisch:* guten Tag!
book [bʊk] *das* Buch
bottle [ˈbɒtl] *die* Flasche
box [bɒks] *die* Schachtel, *die* Kiste
boy [bɔɪ] *der* Junge
bread [bred] *das* Brot
breakfast [ˈbrekfəst] *das* Frühstück
British [ˈbrɪtɪʃ] *der* Brite, *die* Britin; britisch(e, er, es)
brochure [ˈbrəʊʃə] *die* Broschüre, *der* Katalog
broken [ˈbrəʊkən] gebrochen
brother [ˈbrʌðə] *der* Bruder
brown [braʊn] braun
burn [bɜːn] brennen
busy [ˈbɪzɪ] beschäftigt, geschäftig
but [bʌt] aber
bye! [baɪ] *umgangssprachlich:* wiedersehen!, tschüs!

C

cake [keɪk] *der* Kuchen
calculator [ˈkælkjʊleɪtə] *der* Taschenrechner
calendar [ˈkæləndə] *der* Kalender
came (to come) [keɪm (kʌm)] kam (-st, -en)
camera [ˈkæmərə] *die* Kamera, *der* Fotoapparat
camping [ˈkæmpɪŋ] *das* Zelten, *das* Campen
can [kæn, kən] können: **I can't (cannot)** ich kann nicht
cap [kæp] *die* Kappe, *die* Mütze
car [kɑː] *das* Auto
card [kɑːd] *die* Karte
carnival [ˈkɑːnɪvl] *der* Karneval, *der* Fasching
cassette [kəˈset] *die* Kassette
cassette-recorder [kəˈsetrɪˌkɔːdə] *der* Kassettenrekorder
castle [ˈkɑːsl] *die* Burg, *das* Schloss
CD (compact disc) [siːˈdiː (ˌkɒmpækt ˈdɪsk)] *die* CD
centre [ˈsentə] *das* Zentrum, *das* Center
chair [tʃeə] *der* Stuhl
chemists [ˈkemɪsts] *die* Drogerie
child *(Mz:* children) [tʃaɪld (ˈtʃɪldrən)] *das* Kind
chips *(Mz)* [tʃɪps] *die* Pommes frites
chocolate [ˈtʃɒklət] *die* Schokolade
Christmas [ˈkrɪsməs] Weihnachten: Christmas carol *das* Weihnachtslied
church [tʃɜːtʃ] *die* Kirche
cigarette [sɪgəˈret] *die* Zigarette
class [klɑːs] *die* Klasse
classroom [ˈklɑːsrʊm] *das* Klassenzimmer
clever [ˈklevə] klug, schlau
clock [klɒk] *die* (Stand-, Wand)Uhr: **it's ... o'clock** es ist ... Uhr
close [kləʊz] zumachen: closed schloss (-est, -en)
closed [kləʊzd] geschlossen
clown [klaʊn] *der* Clown

one hundred and fifty-nine 159

Dictionary

club [klʌb] *der* Club
coat [kəʊt] *der* Mantel
code [kəʊd] *die* Geheimschrift
coffee ['kɒfɪ] *der* Kaffee
coin [kɔɪn] *die* Münze
cold [kəʊld] kalt
colour ['kʌlə] *die* Farbe: what colour is/are …? welche Farbe hat/haben …?
come from ['kʌm frəm] kommen aus/von
come in [kʌm ˌɪn] hereinkommen
complete [kəm'pliːt] vervollständigen, ergänzen
computer [kəm'pjuːtə] *der* Computer
Computer Studies [kəm'pjuːtə ˌstʌdɪz] Informatik
concertina [kɒnsə'tiːnə] *die* Ziehharmonika
control [kən'trəʊl]: in control of Kontrolle über
corner shop [ˌkɔːnə 'ʃɒp] kleiner Laden an der Ecke, „Tante-Emma-Laden"
cousin ['kʌzn] *der* Cousin, *die* Cousine
crash [kræʃ] *der* Crash
cross [krɒs] überqueren
crow [krəʊ] *die* Krähe
cup [kʌp] *die* Tasse: a cup of tea eine Tasse Tee
cupboard ['kʌbəd] *der* (Küchen-)Schrank

D

dad [dæd] *der* Vater, *der* Vati
dance [dɑːns] tanzen
dangerous ['deɪndʒərəs] gefährlich
date [deɪt] *das* Datum
daughter ['dɔːtə] *die* Tochter
day [deɪ] *der* Tag: one day eines Tages
December [dɪ'sembə] *der* Dezember
desk [desk] *der* Schreibtisch
difference ['dɪfrəns] *der* Unterschied
different ['dɪfrənt] anders
dinner ['dɪnə] *das* Abendessen
do [duː] tun, machen: do the shopping Einkäufe machen
dog [dɒg] *der* Hund
door [dɔː] *die* Tür

double ['dʌbl] doppelt, *hier:* zweimal
drama ['drɑːmə] Drama, Schauspiel
draw [drɔː] zeichnen
drawing ['drɔːɪŋ] *die* Zeichnung
dress [dres] *das* Kleid
drink [drɪŋk] *das* Getränk

E

early ['ɜːlɪ] früh
easy ['iːzɪ] einfach
eat [iːt] essen
eight [eɪt] acht
eighty ['eɪtɪ] achtzig
8.05 (eight oh-five) ['eɪt əʊ 'faɪv] 8 Uhr 05
8.30 (eight thirty) ['eɪt 'θɜːtɪ] 8 Uhr 30
electrical shop [ɪˌlektrɪkl 'ʃɒp] *das* Elektrogeschäft
elephant ['elɪfənt] *der* Elefant
eleven [ɪ'levn] elf
English ['ɪŋglɪʃ] englisch(e, er, es): I'm not English ich bin kein Engländer/keine Engländerin
English teacher ['ɪŋglɪʃ ˌtiːtʃə] *der/die* Englischlehrer(in)
evening ['iːvnɪŋ] *der* Abend
every ['evrɪ] jede(r, s)
everybody ['evrɪbɒdɪ] jeder, alle
excuse me [ɪk'skjuːz miː] entschuldige/entschuldigen Sie, Verzeihung
exercise ['eksəsaɪz] *die* Übung
expensive [ɪk'spensɪv] teuer
eye [aɪ] *das* Auge

F

family ['fæməlɪ] *die* Familie
fantastic [fæn'tæstɪk] fantastisch
far [fɑː] fern
farm [fɑːm] *die* Farm, *der* Bauernhof
father ['fɑːðə] *der* Vater
favourite ['feɪvərɪt] liebstes, Lieblings-
February ['februərɪ] *der* Februar
ferry (*Mz:* ferries) ['ferɪ ('ferɪz)] *die* Fähre
festival ['festɪvəl] *das* Festival, *das* Fest
fetch [fetʃ] holen
few [fjuː]: a few ein paar
fifty ['fɪftɪ] fünfzig

film [fɪlm] *der* Film
find [faɪnd] finden
fine [faɪn]: I'm fine mir geht es gut/ausgezeichnet
finger ['fɪŋgə] *der* Finger
finish ['fɪnɪʃ] aufhören, zu Ende gehen
fire ['faɪə] *das* Feuer
first [fɜːst] erste(r, s)
fish [fɪʃ] *der/die* Fisch(e)
fisherman ['fɪʃəmən] *der* Fischer
fitness ['fɪtnəs] Fitness
five [faɪv] fünf
flat [flæt] platt
flat [flæt] *die* Wohnung
flower ['flaʊə] *die* Blume
fly away [flaɪˌə'weɪ] wegfliegen
folk music ['fəʊk ˌmjuːzɪk] *die* Folkmusik
food [fuːd] *das* Futter, *die* Nahrung, *die* Lebensmittel
foot [fʊt] *der* Fuß
football ['fʊtbɔːl] Fußball
for [fɔː] für
forget [fə'get] vergessen
forty ['fɔːtɪ] vierzig
forty-five ['fɔːtɪfaɪv] fünfundvierzig
four [fɔː] vier
fourteen [fɔː'tiːn] vierzehn
fox [fɒks] *der* Fuchs
free [friː] kostenlos
French [frentʃ] *der* Franzose, *die* Französin; französisch(e, er, es)
Friday ['fraɪdɪ] Freitag
friend [frend] *der/die* Freund(in)
from [frɒm, frəm] von
fun [fʌn] *der* Spaß: judo is fun Judo macht Spaß
funfair ['fʌnfeə] *der* Rummelplatz
funny ['fʌnɪ] lustig; komisch

G

Gaelic ['geɪlɪk, 'gælɪk] gälisch (schottische Minderheitssprache)
game [geɪm] *das* Spiel
garden ['gɑːdn] *der* Garten
German ['dʒɜːmən] *der* Deutsche, *die* Deutsche; deutsch(e, er, es)
get [get] holen
get into [get ˌɪntə] hineinkommen
ghost [gəʊst] *der* Geist, *das* Gespenst

Dictionary

girl [gɜːl] *das* Mädchen
give [gɪv] geben
glad [glæd] froh
go [gəʊ] gehen
go back to [gəʊ ˈbæk tə] zurückgehen zu
go down [gəʊ ˈdaʊn] hinuntergehen
go on to [gəʊ ˈɒn tə] weitergehen zu
good [gʊd] gut: **good at** gut (in)
good morning! [gʊd ˈmɔːnɪŋ] guten Morgen!
good night! [gʊd ˈnaɪt] gute Nacht!
goodbye! [gʊdˈbaɪ] auf Wiedersehen!
grandma [ˈgrænmɑː] *umgangssprachlich: die* Großmutter, *die* Oma
great [greɪt] großartig
Greek [griːk] *der* Grieche, *die* Griechin; griechisch(e, er, es)
green [griːn] grün
greengrocer [ˈgriːngrəʊsə] *der* Gemüsehändler: go into the greengrocer's in den Gemüseladen geh'n
grey [greɪ] grau
group [gruːp] *die* Gruppe
guess [ges] raten

H

half [hɑːf]: **half past seven** halb acht
hall [hɔːl] *das* Herrenhaus, *das* Schloss
hamburger [ˈhæmbɜːgə] *der* Hamburger
hamster [ˈhæmstə] *der* Hamster
hand [hænd] *die* Hand
handbag [ˈhændbæg] *die* Handtasche
happen [ˈhæpən] passieren
happy [ˈhæpɪ] froh; glücklich
hat [hæt] *der* Hut
hate [heɪt] nicht mögen, hassen
have got to [hæv ˈgɒt tə] müssen
have you got? [hæv juː ˈgɒt] hast du?
he [hiː] er: **he's** er ist
he has got [ˌhiː həz ˈgɒt] er hat: **he hasn't got** er hat nicht/kein(e, en)
he won't [hɪ ˈwəʊnt] er wird nicht
head [hed] *der* Kopf

hello! [həˈləʊ] hallo!, guten Tag!
help [help] *die* Hilfe
help [help] helfen
her [hɜː] ihr(e); sie *(persönl. Fürwort, Einzahl)*
here [hɪə] hier, da: **here you are** bitte schön
hey! [heɪ] he!, heda!
hi! [haɪ] hallo!
hill [hɪl] *der* Hügel
him [hɪm] ihn
his [hɪz] sein(e)
hit [hɪt] *der* Hit
hobby *(Mz:* hobbies) [ˈhɒbɪ (ˈhɒbɪz)] *das* Hobby
home [həʊm]: **at home** zu Hause
homework [ˈhəʊmwɜːk] *die* Hausaufgabe(n)
honey [ˈhʌnɪ] *der* Honig
hot [hɒt] heiß
hotdog [ˈhɒtdɒg] *der* Hotdog
hotel [həʊˈtel] *das* Hotel
house [haʊs] *das* Haus
housewife *(Mz:* housewives) [ˈhaʊswaɪf (ˈhaʊswaɪvz)] *die* Hausfrau
how? [haʊ] wie?: **how are you?** wie geht es dir/Ihnen?; **how many?** wie viele?; **how much is …?** wie viel kostet …?; **how old?** wie alt?
hundred [ˈhʌndrɪd] hundert: a/one hundred (ein)hundert
hungry [ˈhʌŋgrɪ] hungrig
hunter [ˈhʌntə] *der* Jäger
hurt [hɜːt] wehtun, verletzen
hurt [hɜːt] verletzt

I

I [aɪ] ich: **I am** ich bin; **I'm** ich bin
I've got [aɪv ˈgɒt] ich habe
idea [aɪˈdɪə] *die* Idee, *der* Einfall
in [ɪn] in: **in English** auf Englisch
Indian [ˈɪndjən] *der* Inder, *die* Inderin; indisch(e, er, es)
interview [ˈɪntəvjuː] *das* Interview
into [ˈɪntʊ] in … hinein
intro(duction) [ˌɪntrəˈdʌkʃn] *die* Einleitung
it [ɪt] es: **it's** es ist
Italian [ɪˈtæljən] *der* Italiener, *die* Italienerin; italienisch(e, er, es)
its [ɪts] ihr(e), sein(e) *(sächlich)*

J

jacket [ˈdʒækɪt] *die* Jacke, *das* Jackett
January [ˈdʒænjʊərɪ] *der* Januar
jar [dʒɑː] *das* Glas, *der* Glasbehälter: a jar of coffee ein Glas Kaffee
jeans *(Mz)* [dʒiːnz] *die* Jeans
job [dʒɒb] *der* Job, *die* Stelle
judo [ˈdʒuːdəʊ] Judo
July [dʒʊˈlaɪ] *der* Juli
June [dʒuːn] *der* Juni

K

kilt [kɪlt] *der* Kilt, *der* Schottenrock
knock [nɒk] *das* Klopfen
know [nəʊ] kennen, wissen: I don't know ich weiß nicht

L

lady [ˈleɪdɪ] *die* Dame
last [lɑːst] letzte(r, s)
late [leɪt] (zu) spät: later später
lead [liːd] anführen
learn [lɜːn] lernen
left [left] links: **on the left** auf der linken Seite
leg [leg] *das* Bein
let [let]: let me … lass mich …; **let's go** lass(t) uns gehen, gehen wir; let's say it lass(t) es uns sagen
letter [ˈletə] *der* Brief
letter [ˈletə] *der* Buchstabe
like [laɪk] mögen, gern haben: I'd like ich möchte bitte, ich hätte gern; like best am liebsten mögen
like this [laɪk ˈðɪs] so, folgendermaßen
list [lɪst] *die* Liste
listen to [ˈlɪsn tə] hören (auf), zuhören
little [ˈlɪtl] klein(er, es)
live [lɪv] wohnen, leben
look at [ˈlʊk ət] anschauen, ansehen
look for [ˈlʊk fə] suchen
lot [lɒt]: a lot of viele
love [lʌv] lieben, gern mögen
lunch [lʌntʃ] *das* Mittagessen

Dictionary

M

madam ['mædəm] gnädige Frau (Anrede)
made in ['meɪd ˌɪn] hergestellt in
magazine [mægə'ziːn] *die* Zeitschrift
magic ['mædʒɪk] magisch, Zauber-
make [meɪk] machen
man (*Mz:* **men**) [mæn (men)] *der* Mann
March [mɑːtʃ] *der* März
match (*Mz:* **matches**) [mætʃ ('mætʃɪz)] *das* Streichholz, *das* Zündholz
match [mætʃ] kombinieren
Maths [mæθs] *die* Mathe(matik)
matter ['mætə]: what's the matter? was ist los?
May [meɪ] *der* Mai
maybe ['meɪbɪ] vielleicht
merry ['merɪ] fröhlich
message ['mesɪdʒ] *die* Botschaft
midnight ['mɪdnaɪt] *die* Mitternacht: at midnight um Mitternacht
milk [mɪlk] *die* Milch
Miss [mɪs] Fräulein (Anrede)
miss [mɪs] vermissen
miss [mɪs] aussetzen
missing ['mɪsɪŋ]: what's missing? was fehlt?
Monday ['mʌndɪ] Montag
money ['mʌnɪ] *das* Geld
monkey ['mʌŋkɪ] *der* Affe
month [mʌnθ] *der* Monat
morning ['mɔːnɪŋ] *der* Morgen: in the morning am Morgen
mother ['mʌðə] *die* Mutter
mouth [maʊθ] *der* Mund
move [muːv] ziehen
Mr ['mɪstə] Herr (Anrede)
Mrs ['mɪsɪz] Frau (Anrede für verheiratete Frauen)
mum [mʌm] *die* Mutter, *die* Mutti
music ['mjuːzɪk] *die* Musik
must [mʌst] müssen
my [maɪ] mein(e)

N

name [neɪm] *der* Name: my name is mein Name ist, ich heiße; **what's your name?** wie ist dein/Ihr Name?, wie heißt du?, wie heißen Sie?

near [nɪə] in der Nähe von, nahe bei
need [niːd] brauchen
neighbour ['neɪbə] *der/die* Nachbar(in)
new [njuː] neu
news (*Mz*) [njuːz] *die* Nachrichten
newsagent ['njuːzeɪdʒənt] *der* Zeitungshändler: go into the newsagent's zum Zeitungshändler gehen
newspaper ['njuːspeɪpə] *die* Zeitung
next [nekst] nächste(r, s)
nice [naɪs] nett
night [naɪt] *die* Nacht: 'night! *umgangssprachlich:* gute Nacht!
nine [naɪn] neun
ninety ['naɪntɪ] neunzig
no [nəʊ] nein: no more keine … mehr
nose [nəʊz] *die* Nase
not [nɒt] nicht
note [nəʊt] *die* Notiz
November [nəʊ'vembə] *der* November
now [naʊ] jetzt; also, nun
number ['nʌmbə] *die* Zahl, *die* Nummer

O

October [ɒk'təʊbə] *der* Oktober
of [ɒv, əv] von
of course [əv 'kɔːs] selbstverständlich
often ['ɒfn] oft
oh! [əʊ] so!, ach!: oh dear! oh je!; oh no! ach du Schande!
okay [əʊ'keɪ] in Ordnung
old [əʊld] alt
on [ɒn] auf
one [wʌn] eins
only ['əʊnlɪ] nur
open ['əʊpən] öffnen, aufmachen: opened öffnete (-st, -n)
open ['əʊpən] geöffnet
opinion [ə'pɪnjən] *die* Meinung
or [ɔː] oder
originally [ə'rɪdʒənəlɪ] ursprünglich
other ['ʌðə] andere(r, s)
our ['aʊə] unser(e, er, es)

P

packet ['pækɪt] *die* Packung: a packet of tea eine Packung Tee

paper ['peɪpə] *das* Papier
parade [pə'reɪd] *die* Parade, *der* Umzug
pardon? ['pɑːdn] wie bitte?
parents (*Mz*) ['peərənts] *die* Eltern
park [pɑːk] *der* Park
part [pɑːt] *der* Teil
partner ['pɑːtnə] *der/die* Partner(in)
past [pɑːst] nach
pen [pen] *der* Füllfederhalter, *der* Füller
pencil ['pensl] *der* Bleistift
penny (*Mz:* pence) (= p) ['penɪ (pens)] *britische Münzeinheit*
people (*Mz*) ['piːpl] *die* Leute
person ['pɜːsn] *die* Person
pet [pet] *das* Haustier
phone [fəʊn] anrufen, telefonieren
photo(graph) ['fəʊtəʊ ('fəʊtəgrɑːf)] *das* Foto
photographer [fə'tɒgrəfə] *der* Fotograf
Physical Education (= P.E.) [ˌfɪzɪkl ˌedjʊ'keɪʃn (piː iː)] Sport, Turnen
piano lesson [pɪ'ænəʊ ˌlesən] *die* Klavierstunde
picnic ['pɪknɪk] *das* Picknick
picture ['pɪktʃə] *das* Bild: in the picture auf dem Bild
piece [piːs] *das* Stück: a piece of paper ein Blatt Papier, ein Zettel
pink [pɪŋk] pink
pity ['pɪtɪ]: what a pity! wie schade!
play [pleɪ] spielen
please [pliːz] bitte
pocket ['pɒkɪt] *die* Tasche (an Kleidungsstücken)
pop music ['pɒp ˌmjuːzɪk] *die* Popmusik
port [pɔːt] *der* Hafen
post office ['pəʊst ˌɒfɪs] *das* Postamt
poster ['pəʊstə] *das* Poster, *das* Plakat
postman ['pəʊstmən] *der* Postbote, *die* Postbotin; *der/die* Briefträger(in)
pound (£) [paʊnd] *das* Pfund (brit. Währung)
problem ['prɒbləm] *das* Problem
professor [prə'fesə] *der* Professor

Dictionary

pub [pʌb] *die* Kneipe, *das* Wirtshaus
pullover [ˈpʊləʊvə] *der* Pullover
pump [pʌmp] *die* (Luft-)Pumpe
pupil [ˈpjuːpl] *der/die* Schüler(in)
put [pʊt] setzen, legen
put on [pʊt ˈɒn] anziehen

Q

quarter [ˈkwɔːtə]: **a quarter to nine** Viertel vor *neun*
question [ˈkwestʃən] *die* Frage: **ask questions** Fragen stellen
quick [kwɪk] schnell
quiz [kwɪz] *das* Quiz

R

ran away (to run away) [ræn əˈweɪ (rʌn əˈweɪ)] rannte (-st, -n) weg
read [riːd] lesen
reader [ˈriːdə] *der/die* Leser(in)
really [ˈrɪəlɪ] eigentlich, wirklich: **not really** eigentlich nicht
recycling [rɪˈsaɪklɪŋ] *das* Recycling
red [red] rot
Religious Education (= R.E.) [rɪˌlɪdʒəs edjʊˈkeɪʃn (ɑː iː)] *der* Religionsunterricht
report [rɪˈpɔːt] *der* Bericht
revision [rɪˈvɪʒn] *die* Wiederholung
rhyme [raɪm] *der* Reim, *der* Vers
riddle [ˈrɪdl] *das* Rätsel
right [raɪt] richtig: **all right** ganz gut, in Ordnung
right [raɪt] rechts: **on the right** auf der rechten Seite
rise up [raɪz ˈʌp] sich aufbäumen
road [rəʊd] *die* Straße
robot [ˈrɒbɒt] *der* Roboter
room [ruːm (rʊm)] *das* Zimmer
rubber [ˈrʌbə] *der* Radiergummi
run [rʌn] rennen, laufen

S

said (to say) [sed (seɪ)] sagte (-st, -n)
sailor [ˈseɪlə] *der* Matrose, *der* Seemann
Saturday [ˈsætədɪ] Sonnabend, Samstag
saw (to see) [sɔː (siː)] sah (-st, -en)
say [seɪ] sagen: **say hello** grüßen, einen Gruß ausrichten
scene [siːn] *die* Szene
school [skuːl] *die* Schule
school bag [ˈskuːl bæg] *die* Schultasche, -mappe
Science [ˈsaɪəns] Naturwissenschaften
Scots [skɒts] *die* Schotten
Scottish [ˈskɒtɪʃ] *der* Schotte, *die* Schottin; schottisch(e, er, es)
scream [skriːm] schreien, kreischen
sea [siː] *das* Meer
seagull [ˈsiːgʌl] *die* Seemöwe
season [ˈsiːzn] *die* Jahreszeit
second [ˈsekənd] zweite(r, s)
see [siː] sehen: **I see** (ich) verstehe, ah ja
sell [sel] verkaufen
sentence [ˈsentəns] *der* Satz
September [sepˈtembə] *der* September
seven [ˈsevn] sieben
seventy [ˈsevntɪ] siebzig
she [ʃiː] sie: **she's** sie ist; **she isn't** sie ist nicht
ship [ʃɪp] *das* Schiff
shirt [ʃɜːt] *das* Hemd
shoe [ʃuː] *der* Schuh
shop [ʃɒp] *der* Laden, *das* Geschäft
shopping day [ˈʃɒpɪŋ deɪ] *der* Einkaufstag
shopping list [ˈʃɒpɪŋ lɪst] *die* Einkaufsliste
shouted (to shout) [ˈʃaʊtɪd (ʃaʊt)] rief (-st, -en), schrie (-st, -n)
show [ʃəʊ] zeigen
shut up [ʃʌt ˈʌp] ruhig sein, den Mund halten
silly [ˈsɪlɪ] dumm, albern
sing [sɪŋ] singen
sir [sɜː] mein Herr *(Anrede)*
sister [ˈsɪstə] *die* Schwester
sit [sɪt] sitzen
sit down [sɪt ˈdaʊn] sich (hin)setzen
six [sɪks] sechs
sixty [ˈsɪkstɪ] sechzig
skirt [skɜːt] *der* Rock
sleep [sliːp] schlafen
small [smɔːl] klein: **smaller** kleiner
smart [smɑːt] schick
so [səʊ] so, also
sock [sɒk] *die* Socke
some [sʌm] etwas
sometimes [ˈsʌmtaɪmz] manchmal
son [sʌn] *der* Sohn
song [sɒŋ] *das* Lied
soon [suːn] bald
sorry! [ˈsɒrɪ] Entschuldigung!, Verzeihung!: **I'm sorry** es tut mir leid, Verzeihung
sound [saʊnd] *der* Laut, *der* Klang
speak [spiːk] sprechen
spell [spel] buchstabieren
sport [spɔːt] *der* Sport
spring [sprɪŋ] *der* Frühling
square [skweə] *das* Quadrat
squash [skwɒʃ] Squash
stall [stɔːl] *die* Bude
stand up [stænd ˈʌp] aufstehen
start [stɑːt] anfangen
station [ˈsteɪʃn] *der* Bahnhof
stay [steɪ] bleiben
step [step] *der* Schritt
stereo [ˈsterɪəʊ] *die* Stereoanlage
stick [stɪk] anheften, kleben
stop [stɒp] aufhören
story [ˈstɔːrɪ] *die* Geschichte
street [striːt] *die* Straße
subject [ˈsʌbdʒekt] *das* Schulfach
sugar [ˈʃʊgə] *der* Zucker
summer [ˈsʌmə] *der* Sommer
Sunday [ˈsʌndɪ] Sonntag
super [ˈsuːpə] super
supermarket [ˈsuːpəmɑːkɪt] *der* Supermarkt
survey [ˈsɜːveɪ] *die* Umfrage
sweets *(Mz)* [swiːts] *die* Süßigkeiten
swimming [ˈswɪmɪŋ] *das* Schwimmen
swimming pool [ˈswɪmɪŋ ˌpuːl] *das* Schwimmbad, -becken

T

T-shirt [ˈtiːʃɜːt] *das* T-Shirt
table [ˈteɪbl] *der* Tisch
take [teɪk] nehmen: **take a photo** ein Foto machen
talk [tɔːk] *das* Gespräch
talk about [ˈtɔːk əˌbaʊt] sprechen über/von
task [tɑːsk] *die* Aufgabe
tea [tiː] *der* Tee
teacher [ˈtiːtʃə] *der/die* Lehrer(in)
team [tiːm] *die* Mannschaft, *das* Team
teatime [ˈtiːtaɪm] *die* Teestunde

Dictionary

teddy bear [ˈtedɪ beə] *der* Teddybär
telephone [ˈtelɪfəʊn] *das* Telefon
telephone number [ˈtelɪfəʊn ˌnʌmbə] *die* Telefonnummer
television [ˈtelɪvɪʒn] *der* Fernseher
tell about [ˈtel‿əˌbaʊt] erzählen von
ten [ten] zehn
tennis [ˈtenɪs] Tennis
terrible [ˈterəbl] schrecklich, furchtbar
test [test] prüfen, testen
text [tekst] *der* Text
than [ðæn, ðən] als *(Vergleich)*
thank you [ˈθæŋk jʊ] danke
thanks [θæŋks] danke
that [ðæt] der, die, das (da); jene(r, s): that's das ist
that's six pounds [ðæts ˌsɪks ˈpaʊndz] das kostet/macht sechs Pfund
the [ðə] der, die, das
their [ðeə] ihr(e) *(Mz)*
then [ðen] dann, also
there [ðeə] dort, da: there are es gibt, da sind; there is es gibt, da ist; there's es gibt, da ist
they [ðeɪ] sie *(Mz)*: they're sie sind
they've got [ðeɪv ˈɡɒt] sie haben
thing [θɪŋ] *das* Ding, *die* Sache: things are fine alles läuft gut
think [θɪŋk] nachdenken, überlegen
third [θɜːd] dritte(r, s)
thirteen [θɜːˈtiːn] dreizehn
thirty [ˈθɜːtɪ] dreißig
thirty-five [ˈθɜːtɪfaɪv] fünfunddreißig
this [ðɪs] diese(r, s); das
thought (to think) [θɔːt (θɪŋk)] dachte (-st, -n)
three [θriː] drei
Thursday [ˈθɜːzdɪ] Donnerstag: on Thursdays donnerstags
till [tɪl] bis
time [taɪm] *die* Zeit: have a great time sich amüsieren, großen Spaß haben; what's the time? wie viel Uhr ist es?
tin [tɪn] *die* Büchse, *die* Dose
tired [ˈtaɪəd] müde
to [tə] zu(m); vor
today [təˈdeɪ] heute
together [təˈɡeðə] zusammen, miteinander
too [tuː] auch

tourist [ˈtʊərɪst] *der* Tourist
town [taʊn] *die* Stadt
toy [tɔɪ] *das* Spielzeug
traditional [trəˈdɪʃənəl] traditionell, überliefert
traffic lights *(Mz)* [ˈtræfɪk laɪts] *die* Ampel
tree [triː] *der* Baum
trousers *(Mz)* [ˈtraʊzəz] *die* Hose
Tuesday [ˈtjuːzdɪ] Dienstag
Turkish [ˈtɜːkɪʃ] *der* Türke, *die* Türkin; türkisch(e, er, es)
turn [tɜːn] *die* Runde: it's your turn du bist an der Reihe
turn [tɜːn] abbiegen
TV [tiːˈviː] *der* Fernsehapparat
twelve [twelv] zwölf
twenty [ˈtwentɪ] zwanzig
twenty-one [ˌtwentɪˈwʌn] einundzwanzig
twenty-two oh-two [ˈtewntɪtuːəʊˈtuː] 22 Uhr 02
two [tuː] zwei
tyre [ˈtaɪə] *der* Reifen: flat tyre *die* Reifenpanne, *der* Platten

U

uncle [ˈʌŋkl] *der* Onkel
under [ˈʌndə] unter
uniform [ˈjuːnɪfɔːm] *die* Uniform
unit [ˈjuːnɪt] *die* Lektion
up [ʌp] oben
us [ʌs] uns

V

vegetables *(Mz)* [ˈvedʒtəblz] *das* Gemüse
very [ˈverɪ] sehr
video [ˈvɪdɪəʊ] *das* Video(gerät)
video shop [ˈvɪdɪəʊ ˌʃɒp] *das* Videogeschäft
violet [ˈvaɪələt] violett
visit [ˈvɪzɪt] besuchen
volleyball [ˈvɒlɪbɔːl] Volleyball

W

wait [weɪt] warten
walk [wɔːk] gehen
wall [wɔːl] *die* Wand
want [wɒnt] wollen, wünschen
warm [wɔːm] warm
was [wɒz, wəz] war *(Vergangenheit)*
wash [wɒʃ] waschen
watch [wɒtʃ] beobachten, ansehen

watch TV (= *television*) [ˌwɒtʃ tiːˈviː] fernsehen
water [ˈwɔːtə] *das* Wasser
way [weɪ] *der* Weg: we're on our way wir sind auf dem Weg
we [wiː] wir: we aren't wir sind nicht/keine; we'll wir werden; we're wir sind; we shall wir sollen
we've got [wiːv ˈɡɒt] wir haben
wear [weə] *(Kleidung)* tragen, anhaben
Wednesday [ˈwenzdɪ] Mittwoch
week [wiːk] *die* Woche
welcome to [ˈwelkəm tə] willkommen in/im
well [wel] also
what? [wɒt] was?: what's …? was ist …?; what are they saying? was sagen sie?
what about …? [ˈwɒt‿əˌbaʊt] was ist mit …?, wie steht es mit …?
when [wen] wenn
when? [wen] wann?
where? [weə] wo?; wohin?: where's? wo ist?
white [waɪt] weiß
who? [huː] wer?: who's? wer ist?
whoo-hoo! [ˈwuːhuː] Juhu!
whose? [huːz] wessen?
window [ˈwɪndəʊ] *das* Fenster
winner [ˈwɪnə] *der/die* Gewinner(in), *der/die* Sieger(in)
winter [ˈwɪntə] *der* Winter
wish [wɪʃ] wünschen
with [wɪð] mit
woman (*Mz:* women) [ˈwʊmən (ˈwɪmɪn)] *die* Frau
wonderful [ˈwʌndəfʊl] wunderbar
wood [wʊd] *der* Wald
word [wɜːd] *das* Wort
work [wɜːk] arbeiten
worm [wɜːm] *der* Wurm
write about [ˈraɪt‿əˌbaʊt] schreiben über
wrong [rɒŋ] falsch

Y

year [jɪə] *das* Jahr
yellow [ˈjeləʊ] gelb
yes [jes] ja
you [juː] du, Sie, ihr; dir, dich/euch, euch/Ihnen, Sie: you are du bist, Sie sind; you're du bist
you've got [juːv ˈɡɒt] du hast
your [jɔː] dein(e), Ihr(e)

Fact Finder

In diesem Fact Finder findest du die Namen der wichtigsten Orte, Länder und Regionen, Einrichtungen, Sehenswürdigkeiten und Personen dieses Buches.

In der linken Spalte steht jeweils – in alphabetischer Reihenfolge – die englische Bezeichnung und die korrekte Aussprache, in der rechten Spalte werden die Namen erklärt.

Du erfährst hier also ganz nebenbei noch interessante Dinge und "Facts" über Großbritannien und die englischsprachige Welt.

Alexandra Park [ˌælɪgˈzɑːndrə ˌpɑːk]	Name eines Parks
All Saints' Day [ˌɔːl ˈseɪnts deɪ]	Allerheiligen
Allaway Avenue [ˌæləweɪ ˈævənjuː]	Straßenname
Ankara [ˈæŋkərə]	Hauptstadt der Türkei
BBC (= British Broadcasting Corporation) [biːbiːˈsiː (ˈbrɪtɪʃ ˈbrɔːdkɑːstɪŋ kɔːpəˈreɪʃn)]	öffentlich-rechtliches Fernsehen in Großbritannien
Britain [ˈbrɪtn]	Großbritannien
Bruce Willis [ˌbruːs ˈwɪlɪs]	amerik. Filmstar
Castle Street [ˈkɑːsl ˌstriːt]	Straßenname
Coco [ˈkəʊkəʊ]	Spitzname
Cosham [ˈkɒʃəm]	Ort bei Portsmouth
Crickwood [ˈkrɪkwʊd]	Ort bei Portsmouth
Dallas [ˈdæləs]	Stadt in Texas, USA
Demi Moore [ˈdemɪ ˈmɔː]	amerik. Filmstar
Dracula [ˈdrækjʊlə]	Name eines berühmten Vampirs
Dublin [ˈdʌblɪn]	Hauptstadt der Republik Irland
Edinburgh [ˈedɪnbərə]	Hauptstadt von Schottland
Europe [ˈjʊərəp]	Europa
Fareham [ˈfeərəm]	Ort bei Portsmouth
France [frɑːns]	Frankreich
Frankenstein [ˈfræŋkənstaɪn]	Hauptfigur im gleichnamigen Buch
Fuzzy Wuzzy [ˌfʌzɪ ˈwʌzɪ]	Name eines Bärs
GB (Great Britain) [ˌdʒiː ˈbiː (ˌgreɪt ˈbrɪtn)]	Großbritannien
Glasgow [ˈglɑːsgəʊ]	Großstadt in Schottland
Glenmore [glenˈmɔː]	Teil des schottischen Hochlandes
Goodfood [ˈgʊdfuːd]	Name eines Restaurants
Grove Road [ˈgrəʊv ˌrəʊd]	Straßenname
Halloween [ˌhæləʊˈiːn]	Fest in englischsprachigen Ländern am 31. Oktober
Highbury [ˈhaɪbərɪ]	Ort bei Portsmouth
Hilsea [ˈhɪlsiː]	Ort bei Portsmouth
Hong Kong [ˈhɒŋ ˈkɒŋ]	chinesische Provinz
Inverness [ɪnvəˈnes]	Stadt in Schottland
King Street [ˈkɪŋ striːt]	Straßenname
Kristy and the snobs [ˈkrɪstɪ ənd ðə ˈsnɒbz]	Buchtitel
Loch Ness [lɒx ˈnes]	See in Schottland
London [ˈlʌndən]	Hauptstadt von Großbritannien
Lord Willis [ˌlɔːd ˈwɪlɪs]	Adeliger
Ludlow [ˈlʌdləʊ]	Stadt in England
Manchester [ˈmæntʃestə]	Großstadt in England
Marsden Road [ˌmɑːzdən ˈrəʊd]	Straßenname
Marsdown [ˈmɑːzdaʊn]	Name
Mountbatten Centre [maʊntˈbætn ˌsentə]	Name eines Freizeitzentrums
Munich [ˈmjɔːnɪk]	München
New York [nʊ ˈjɔːk]	Großstadt in den USA
Ocean Radio [ˈəʊʃn ˈreɪdɪəʊ]	Name einer Radiostation
Paulsgrove [ˈpɔːlsgrəʊv]	Siedlung in Portsmouth
Paulsgrove Club [ˈpɔːlsgrəʊv ˈklʌb]	Bürgerzentrum in Paulsgrove
Pinocchio [pɪˈnəʊkɪəʊ]	Holzpuppe in einer Zeichentrickserie

Fact Finder

Portchester ['pɔːtʃestə]	Stadt in Südengland	**Twirlettes** [twɜːˈlets]	Name einer Marsch- und Tanztruppe
Portsmouth ['pɔːtsməθ]	Hafenstadt in Südengland	**UK (= United Kingdom)** [ˌjuːˈkeɪ (jʊˈnaɪtɪd ˈkɪŋdəm)]	Vereinigtes Königreich
Princes Street ['prɪnsɪz ˌstriːt]	Straße in Edinburgh		
Queen [kwiːn]	Königin von England	**Upton** ['ʌptən]	Städtename
Royal Family [ˌrɔɪəl ˈfæmɪlɪ]	die königliche Familie	**USA (= United States of America)** [jʊˈnaɪtɪd ˈsteɪts əv əˈmerɪkə]	Vereinigte Staaten von Amerika
Scotland ['skɒtlənd]	Schottland		
St. Martin [seɪnt ˈmɑːtɪn]	Martinstag (Fest am 11. November in Deutschland)	**Victory** ['vɪktərɪ]	Schiffsname (wörtlich: Sieg)
Sydney ['sɪdnɪ]	Großstadt in Australien	**Wales** [weɪlz]	Wales
Thanksgiving [ˌθæŋksˈgɪvɪŋ]	Erntedankfest	**Washington** ['wɒʃɪŋtən]	Hauptstadt der USA
The Babysitters Club [ðə ˈbeɪbɪsɪtəz ˌklʌb]	Buchreihe	**West Street** ['west ˌstriːt]	Straßenname
The Green [ðə ˈgriːn]	Name f. Grünfläche (Park) in der Stadtmitte	**Windsor Piano School** ['wɪndzə ˈpjænəʊ ˌskuːl]	Name einer Schule
Toronto [təˈrɒntəʊ]	Großstadt in Kanada		
Totland ['tɒtlənd]	Badeort an der engl. Südküste		

Fact Finder/Names

Girls/Women

Alexandra [ælɪgˈzɑːndrə]
Alice [ˈælɪs]
Alison [ˈælɪsn]
Ann [æn]
Anne [æn]
Barbara [ˈbɑːbrə]
Christina [krɪˈstiːnə]
Cindy [ˈsɪndɪ]
Doris [ˈdɒrɪs]
Elizabeth [ɪˈlɪzəbəθ]
Jane [dʒeɪn]
Julia [ˈdʒuːljə]
Kim [kɪm]
Linda [ˈlɪndə]
Madur [ˈmædʊə]
Margaret [ˈmɑːgrət]
Mary [ˈmeərɪ]
Pam [pæm]
Pat [pæt]
Penny [ˈpenɪ]
Philippa [ˈfɪlɪpə]
Rebecca [rəˈbekə]
Rita [ˈriːtə]
Rosie [ˈrəʊzɪ]
Ruth [ruːθ]
Sally [ˈsælɪ]
Sibylle [sɪˈbɪlə]
Silvia [ˈsɪlvɪə]
Susan [ˈsuːzn]
Susie [ˈsuːzɪ]
Tanja [ˈtænjə]
Tina [ˈtɪnə]

Boys/Men

Alec [ˈælɪk]
Andy [ˈændɪ]
Anton [ˈæntɒn]
Arnold [ˈɑːnld]
Ben [ben]
Bill [bɪl]
Cecil [ˈsesɪl]
Clark [klɑːk]
Dan [dæn]
Dave [deɪv]
David [ˈdeɪvɪd]
Frank [fræŋk]
George [dʒɔːdʒ]
Grant [grɑːnt]
Henry [ˈhenrɪ]
Jim [dʒɪm]
Jimmy [ˈdʒɪmɪ]
Joey [ˈdʒəʊɪ]
John [dʒɒn]
Len [len]
Mark [mɑːk]
Martin [ˈmɑːtɪn]
Michael [ˈmaɪkl]
Mick [mɪk]
Orville [ˈɔːvɪl]
Peter [ˈpiːtə]
Ramesh [ˈræmeʃ]
Rex [reks]
Rick [rɪk]
Rob [rɒb]
Robbie [ˈrɒbɪ]
Robby [ˈrɒbɪ]
Robert [ˈrɒbət]
Sam [sæm]
Simon [ˈsaɪmən]
Stephen [ˈstiːvn]
Stuart [ˈstjʊət]
Willi [ˈwɪlɪ]

Families

Bignall [ˈbɪgnəl]
Carey [ˈkeərɪ]
Carstairs [ˈkɑːsteəz]
Dean [diːn]
Fielding [ˈfiːldɪŋ]
Green [griːn]
Harman [ˈhɑːmən]
Jackson [ˈdʒæksn]
Johnson [ˈdʒɒnsən]
Miller [ˈmɪlə]
Moore [mʊə]
Patel [pəˈtel]
Peters [ˈpiːtəz]
Roberts [ˈrɒbəts]
Roper [ˈrəʊpə]
Ross [rɒs]
Sands [sændz]
Schwarzenegger [ˈʃwɔːtsn,egə]
Smith [smɪθ]
Waits [weɪts]
Willis [ˈwɪlɪs]
Wilson [ˈwɪlsən]

Animals

Dolphy [ˈdɒlfɪ]
Fishy [ˈfɪʃɪ]
Fleet [fliːt]
Fuzzy Wuzzy [ˈfʌzɪ ˌwʌzɪ]
Mr Christian [ˈkrɪstʃən]
Octo [ˈɒktəʊ]
Raffles [ˈræflz]
Skipper [ˈskɪpə]

Numbers, letters, sounds ...

Numbers

1	one	[wʌn]
2	two	[tuː]
3	three	[θriː]
4	four	[fɔː]
5	five	[faɪv]
6	six	[sɪks]
7	seven	[sevn]
8	eight	[eɪt]
9	nine	[naɪn]
10	ten	[ten]
11	eleven	[ɪˈlevn]
12	twelve	[twelv]
13	thirteen	[ˌθɜːˈtiːn]
14	fourteen	[ˌfɔːˈtiːn]
15	fifteen	[ˌfɪfˈtiːn]
16	sixteen	[ˌsɪksˈtiːn]
17	seventeen	[ˌsevnˈtiːn]
18	eighteen	[ˌeɪˈtiːn]
19	nineteen	[ˌnaɪnˈtiːn]
20	twenty	[ˈtewntɪ]
21	twenty-one	[ˌtwentɪˈwʌn]
30	thirty	[ˈθɜːtɪ]
40	forty	[ˈfɔːtɪ]
50	fifty	[ˈfɪftɪ]
60	sixty	[ˈsɪkstɪ]
70	seventy	[ˈsevntɪ]
80	eighty	[ˈeɪtɪ]
90	ninety	[ˈnaɪntɪ]
100	a hundred	[ə ˈhʌndrəd]
	one hundred	[ˌwʌn ˈhʌndrəd]

Days of the week

Monday	[ˈmʌndɪ]
Tuesday	[ˈtjuːzdɪ]
Wednesday	[ˈwenzdɪ]
Thursday	[ˈθɜːzdɪ]
Friday	[ˈfraɪdɪ]
Saturday	[ˈsætədɪ]
Sunday	[ˈsʌndɪ]

Months

January	[ˈdʒænjʊərɪ]
February	[ˈfebrʊərɪ]
March	[ˈmɑːtʃ]
April	[ˈeɪprəl]
May	[meɪ]
June	[dʒuːn]
July	[dʒʊˈlaɪ]
August	[ˈɔːɡəst]
September	[sepˈtembə]
October	[ɒkˈtəʊbə]
November	[nəʊˈvembə]
December	[dɪˈsembə]

Letters

a	[eɪ]	d	[diː]	g	[dʒiː]	j	[dʒeɪ]	m	[em]	p	[piː]	s	[es]	v	[viː]	y	[waɪ]
b	[biː]	e	[iː]	h	[eɪtʃ]	k	[keɪ]	n	[en]	q	[kjuː]	t	[tiː]	w	[ˈdʌbljuː]	z	[zed]
c	[siː]	f	[ef]	i	[aɪ]	l	[el]	o	[əʊ]	r	[ɑː]	u	[juː]	x	[eks]

Sounds

Vowels/Vokale/Selbstlaute

[ɪ] it, six, big
[e] pet, tell, friend
[æ] bad, thanks, man
[ʌ] cup, come, number
[ɒ] what, on, dog
[ʊ] put, look, good
[ə] a sailor, sister, German

[iː] tea, street, please
[ɑː] car, father, garden
[ɔː] door, four, small
[uː] two, food, judo
[ɜː] girl, German, Turkish

[eɪ] name, they, play
[aɪ] nice, fine, five
[ɔɪ] boy, toy
[aʊ] now, house, about
[əʊ] no, know, hello
[ɪə] here, dear, near
[eə] chair, their, there
[ʊə] tourist

Consonants/Konsonanten/Mitlaute

[p] pencil, pump
[b] baby, table, club
[t] tea, street
[d] door, window, food
[k] car, book
[g] girl, again, bag
[f] fine, photo, often
[v] very, have, five
[θ] thanks, month
[ð] this, mother, with
[s] six, cassettes
[z] easy, does, his
[ʃ] she, Scottish
[ʒ] television
[tʃ] chair, teacher, church
[dʒ] German, George
[m] milk, summer, time
[n] no, know, woman
[ŋ] sing, uncle, monkey
[l] letter, yellow, little
[j] yes, new, unit
[w] we, what, twelve, question

[r] read, dress, very
[h] here, who, bighead

[ː] der vorangehende Laut ist lang [tuː]
[ˈ] Hauptbetonung: die folgende Silbe ist betont [ɪˈlevn]
[ˌ] Nebenbetonung: die folgende Silbe ist betont, aber schwächer als beim Hauptton [ˌθɜːˈtiːn]
[‿] die beiden Laute werden verbunden [pʊt‿ɒn]

Classroom talk

What your teacher says

Come in, please.	*Kommt bitte herein.*
Sit down, please.	*Setzt euch bitte.*
Open the window, please.	*Mach bitte das Fenster auf.*
Close the door, please.	*Mach bitte die Türe zu.*
Be quiet, please.	*Seid bitte still.*

Say it again, please.	*Wiederhole das bitte.*
Can you say that in English, please?	*Kannst du das bitte auf Englisch sagen?*

Open your books at page 35, please.	*Schlagt eure Bücher bitte auf Seite 35 auf.*
Where's your homework?	*Wo ist deine Hausaufgabe?*
Write the sentence on the blackboard, please.	*Schreibe bitte den Satz an die Tafel.*
Look at the pictures, please.	*Schaut euch bitte die Bilder an.*
It's your turn now.	*Du bist jetzt an der Reihe.*
Can you do this exercise?	*Kannst du diese Übung machen?*
Go on, please.	*Mach bitte weiter.*
Shut your books, please.	*Macht bitte eure Bücher zu.*

Now work with your partner.	*Nun arbeitet mit eurem Partner.*
Let's do some group work now.	*Wir werden jetzt Gruppenarbeit machen.*
Ask your partner.	*Frage deinen Partner.*
Can you help him/her?	*Kannst du ihm/ihr helfen?*

What you can say

Can you help me, please?	*Können Sie mir bitte helfen?*
Sorry, I don't understand.	*Entschuldigung, ich verstehe das nicht.*
Not so quick, please.	*Nicht so schnell, bitte.*
Can you say that again, please?	*Können Sie das bitte wiederholen?*
Is that right?	*Ist das richtig?*

Sorry. I've got a question.	*Entschuldigung, ich habe eine Frage.*
Can I speak German, please?	*Kann ich bitte deutsch sprechen?*
What's "Buch" in English, please?	*Was heißt „Buch" auf Englisch, bitte?*

Sorry, what's the homework?	*Entschuldigung, was haben wir als Hausaufgabe auf?*

Can I go to the toilet, please?	*Darf ich bitte zur Toilette gehen?*

For partner work

Can we do this together?	*Können wir das zusammen machen?*
Okay, let's work together.	*Gut, arbeiten wir zusammen.*
Let's write …	*Lass uns schreiben …*

That's right./That isn't right.	*Das ist richtig./Das ist nicht richtig.*
That's good	*Das ist gut.*
That's wrong.	*Das ist falsch.*

Acknowledgements

We are grateful to the following for permission to reproduce/use copyright material:

Texts and songs:

Prof. Dr. Gerngroß, Prof. Dr. H. Puchta, Graz, Univ. Doz. Dr. M. Schratz, Innsbruck for " The box of nuts ": page **62** and for " The clever crow " page **89**

Longman Group UK Ltd., Harlow for " Good Morning " from *Jig saw Songs* by Trevor Jones and Brian Abbs: page **4** and for the "ABC song " from *Welcome to English* by Martin Bates: page **95**

Illustrations

Shirley Bellwood(BL Kearly Ltd.): page 56, 98

Celia Canning (Linda Rogers Associates, London: page 100

Erich Ballinger, Stainz: page 57, 58 (middle)

Jürgen Bartz, München: Umschlagseite 2, pages IV, XII, 40 (right), 49 (No 2), 52, 91 (top left), 99, 128 (left)

Erhard Dietl, Ottobrunn: pages 44 (bottom left), 58 (top), 110, 111

Dover Publications, Inc., New York:page 46, 49 (top left:Nos 1, 3, 4), 78 from *Handbook of Pictorial Symbols*

Barbara Köhler, München: page 30, 105

Jörg Plannerer, München: page III , 1 (top), 3 (top right), 5 (middle right), 5 (bottom), 7, 8, 9 (bottom right), 10 (top), 10 (middle), 12 (left), 12 (top right), 13 (bottom), 14 , 16 , 17 , 21 , 23 , 28 , 29 , 34 (middle), 38 (middle), 38 (bottom), 39 (top left), 42 (left), 43 (bottom), 44 (top), 44 (middle), 50 , 54 , 66, 67 (bottom right), 67 (top), 72 , 74 , 76 , 77, 80 (bottom), 82, 83, 84, 90, 91 (top right), 92, 95, 96 (middle left), 96 (bottom), 107, 109, 117 (bottom left), 117 (middle left), 117 (Nos 1,13), 119 (bottom right), 120, 123, 128 (bottom), 130, 132

Peter Stevenson, Linden Artists Ltd, London: page IV, V-XI, 1 (bottom), 2, 3 (top left), 4, 5 (middle left), 5 (top), 6 , 9 (top, middle left, bottom left), 10 (bottom), 11, 12 (bottom right), 13 (top), 15 , 19 , 22 (right),24, 25 (bottom), 26, 27, 32 (top), 32 (bottom right), 33, 35, 36, 37, 39 (top right), 40 (bottom right), 42 (right), 43 (top), 44 (middle), 52, 47, 48, 51, 53, 64, 67 (bottom left), 69-71, 73 (top left), 79, 80 (top), 81, 86-88, 91 (middle right), 93, 97, 103, 112, 114, 115, 117 (Nos 12, 18, 19; top right), 118 (middle, bottom left), 119 (left)

Achim Theil, München: page 1(top), 63

David Vaughan, München: pages 20, 22 (top left), 25 (top), 32 (bottom left), 34 (top, bottom), 38 (top), 39 (bottom), 45 (top), 49 (bottom), 73 (bottom), 79, 82, 94, 96 (middle right), 116, 117 (middle right), 118 (top right/left, bottom right)

Photographs

Cover photograph: Tony Stone Bilderwelten, München

action press, Hamburg: page 99 (left)

Beate Andler-Teufel, München: page 96 (top), 101, 109 (left)

Barnaby's Picture Library, London: page 75, 102 (No 4)

Jürgen Bartz, München: page 68 (Nos 2, 7)

Dr. Siegfried Birle, München: page 68 (No 6)

British Tourist Authority, Frankfurt: page 18 (No 2), 68 (No 5), 102 (No 2,3)

Bulls Press, Frankfurt, page: XII(bottom right)

Dick Castledine, Harlow: page 109 (right)

Central Office of Information, London, page: 18 (Nos 1,6)

Laurence Harger, Nürnberg: page 18 (Nos 3,4,5)

IFA Bilderteam GmbH, München: page 68 (Nos 1,4)

Peter Illmeier, Graz: page 65

The Image Bank Bildagentur, München: page XII (bottom left)

Nick Jones, Bath: page 68 (No 3)

Bettina Lindenberg, München: page VIII (top left), 55 (top)

Bildarchiv Mauritius, Mittenwald: page X (top right), 99 (right)

Terry Moston, Fröndenberg: page 98

Thomas Müller, Darmstadt: page 53 (left)

Nusser-Verlag, München: page 102 (No 1)

W. Rudolph Dia Archiv, München: page 102   (middle)

Tony Stone Bilderwelten, München: page XII (top left)

Visual Publications, London: page 53 (right)

The traditional song." London' s burning " on page 42 was taken from *Songs and Rhymes for the teaching of English* by Julian Dakin, Longman Group UK Ltd, Harlow.

We should be grateful for any information which might assist us in tracing the copyright owners of sources which we have been unable to acknowledge.

Englisch

Pakistan (Pakistan)

India (Indien)

African countries (Afrikanische Länder)

Australia (Australien)

New Zealand (Neuseeland)